ARTIFICIAL INTELLIGENCE:
Applications to Logical Reasoning and Historical Research

ELLIS HORWOOD SERIES IN COMPUTERS AND THEIR APPLICATIONS

Series Editor: Brian Meek, Director of the Computer Unit, Queen Elizabeth College, University of London

ARTIFICIAL INTELLIGENCE:
Applications to Logical Reasoning and Historical Research

RICHARD ENNALS
Research Manager,
Fifth Generation Research Group,
Department of Computing,
Imperial College of Science and Technology,
University of London

ELLIS HORWOOD LIMITED
Publishers · Chichester

Halsted Press: a division of
JOHN WILEY & SONS
Chichester · New York · Ontario · Brisbane

First published in 1985 and
Reprinted in 1986 by
ELLIS HORWOOD LIMITED
Market Cross House, Cooper Street, Chichester, West Sussex, PO19 1EB, England

The publisher's colophon is reproduced from James Gillison's drawing of the ancient Market Cross, Chichester.

Distributors:

Australia, New Zealand, South-east Asia:
Jacaranda-Wiley Ltd., Jacaranda Press,
JOHN WILEY & SONS INC.,
G.P.O. Box 859, Brisbane, Queensland 4001, Australia

Canada:
JOHN WILEY & SONS CANADA LIMITED
22 Worcester Road, Rexdale, Ontario, Canada.

Europe, Africa:
JOHN WILEY & SONS LIMITED
Baffins Lane, Chichester, West Sussex, England.

North and South America and the rest of the world:
Halsted Press: a division of
JOHN WILEY & SONS
605 Third Avenue, New York, N.Y. 10158, U.S.A.

© 1985 J. R. Ennals/Ellis Horwood Limited

British Library Cataloguing in Publication Data
Ennals, J. R.
Artificial Intelligence: Applications to Logical Reasoning and Historical Research
(Ellis Horwood Computers and their Applications series)
1. History — Computer assisted instruction
I. Title
907'.8   D16.255.C6

Library of Congress Card No. 85-804

ISBN 0-85312-856-1 (Ellis Horwood Limited)
ISBN 0-470-20181 (Halsted Press)

Typeset by Ellis Horwood Limited
Printed in Great Britain by R. J. Acford, Chichester

Contents

Preface and acknowledgements

This book has been many years in the making. It addresses problems of understanding in history and the humanities that have been of academic concern for centuries within the confines of a number of different disciplines. Exploring such problems has required the author to be something of a hybrid, and has led him to explore the potential of different media and technologies.

The role of the history teacher has often been appropriate, for teachers have to make themselves expert in diverse fields at different levels and with different modes of expression to their different audiences of individuals and groups. Those who are concerned with the construction of expert systems have a long way to go before they can match the knowledge, skills, and flexibility required of a good history teacher today.

I focus in this book on the role of logic and of logic programming, for it seems to me that here at last we have a generally acceptable notation in which we can describe what we mean, where our description taken as a program can serve to demonstrate what we mean to others.

There has been an Anglo-Saxon tradition of dissociating logic from its area of application, which can be contrasted with the French and continental tradition of seeing logic in terms of articulating domains of discourse. As this book sets out to show, logic programming has roots in both of these traditions, and is increasingly providing a medium through which they can communicate.

Another link between the two traditions can be found in the concern of historians and 'human scientists', or students of 'les sciences de l'homme', to make sense of the world around them, and to make intelligent use of available evidence. I have found the closest links in approach between French social historians and British (and Australian) history teachers in the 'New history' school. This is no coincidence, and in this case many of the links can be established through Cambridge, where the French influences have been strong and the effects on British classroom teaching increasing over the last fifteen years.

Much has changed in the development of the new technology of computer science. A new 'fifth generation' of computers is being developed, with which the author is closely associated. Computer scientists, however, are suddenly realizing that, with all their new computing power, they do not have a theory of knowledge that will allow them sensibly to exploit this power. I believe that there is such a theory of knowledge but that computer scientists do not have it. Scientists have been so concerned with how things work, or with constructing intricate working machines that, I would argue, they have lost sight of how things are, and how we can make sense of our world. The declarative use of logic enables us to take insights of our contemporaries and of our predecessors, and to explore them with new power, interrogating the accounts and extracting explanations. There is a vast literature of scholarship and a history of achievement of endeavour. Computer scientists do not read, and few have studied history.

This book cannot claim to solve all the old problems. What it can offer is suggestions based on research and classroom experience, and a trail of references to the ideas from which further advances should come.

The computer technology used in the work described is cheap and widely available. It is interesting that a language, micro-PROLOG, first developed for use with children on the project 'Logic as a computer language' on which the author has worked since 1980, is now in use around the world on computers of all sizes and manufacture. Before teaching the computer scientists we have first had to learn from the children, and, it should be emphasized, from teachers of history, who have taken the lead in so many research projects in Britain and overseas.

This book does not provide a tutorial introduction to logic programming as such. The author has written one such introduction (Ennals 1984a), contributed to another more advanced introduction (Clark & McCabe 1984), and provided short introductions in many other published works. The focus of attention here are the problems arising in history teaching and artificial intelligence, though many of the example programs have a tutorial function in introducing aspects of logic programming and PROLOG. No previous knowledge of PROLOG is required.

My first paper in this field, 'Shakespeare as a historian', was written in 1967. To acknowledge all of those who have helped and influenced me since then would be impossible, but I should mention in particular, in some kind of chronological order: Patrick Richardson, Frank Miles, Mike Smith, Leonard James, Jim Hopkins, Bernard Williams, Roger Scruton, John Dunn, Hugh Anderson, Christopher Morris, Alan MacFarlane, Don Thompson, Peter Lee, Stephen Frank, John Waddleton, Peter Vance, Martin Frampton, Bob Kowalski, Alan Robinson, Keith Clark, Frank McCabe, Diane Reeve, Marek Sergot, Peter Hammond, Derek Brough, Jonathan Briggs, Jon Nichol, and Mike Horwood.

I should also acknowledge my debt to successive employers: to the London Borough of Merton, Essex County Council, Kano State of Nigeria, and, at Imperial College, to the Science and Engineering Research Council, the Nuffield Foundation, and the Alvey Directorate.

Material in some of the chapters has appeared in some of my previous publications, and this is indicated in the chapters concerned. I am grateful to the Journal editors and to the publishers of the previous versions for their permission.

My real debt is to my family, Bobbie, Robert, and Christopher, who have supported me throughout.

Hampton

August, 1984

1

The use of the computer in the study and teaching of history: possibilities and priorities for the future

1.1 INTRODUCTION

The computer does not have a long history. It has only recently started to make a serious contribution to the study and teaching of history, and should be regarded as a new apprentice in our ancient trade. Apprentices depend for their development into maturity on the advice, wisdom, and practial experience of their more senior colleagues, and traditionally only expect to be described as competent after a period of years. If we want the computer to be useful to us in the study and teaching of history we will have to be prepared to tell it what it is that we do. Computers can follow the guidance of experts who have been prepared to describe the nature of their expertise. The computer itself is not the problem. Its use should be a consequence of the view that we take of our subject and the role that we assign to the computer as a powerful tool.

The above argument does not apply only to practitioners in the study and teaching of history. Historians are, however, at a considerable potential advantage relative to other professions, and have a great deal to contribute not just to the use of computers in their own discipline, but to the future of the intelligent use of computers in general.

In recent years our approach to the teaching of history has been increasingly affected by our approach to the study of history. Behind the 'New History' lies the idea that we should introduce students to history by involving them in the activity of being an historian. A history lesson will itself constitute a simulation, from the point of view of method. The development of this approach and the appropriate teaching materials has involved considerable reflection on the nature of history as a form of knowledge and its particular subject matter, concepts, patterns of reasoning, and modes of confirming conclusions.

Though the computer itself is of recent vintage, it should be seen in the context of a concern for problems of knowledge and reasoning that dates from the time of Socrates. Given the large amount of information to be dealt with, and the complex reasoning involved in understanding a variety of human problems, philosophers and logicians for centuries have longed to have access to machines that could automate reasoning and the processing of large bodies of information. The first forty years of the existence of computers were dominated by the demands of the machine: to be addressed in a special language that it understood, to be presented with a specific sequence of operations to be performed, and preferably to be asked to do things that involve numerical operations. Unsurprisingly, historians showed relatively little interest in a machine that involved them in departing significantly from their view of their subject, emphasizing quantitative rather than qualitative elements. The computer systems that are now being built can return us to the older tradition of a concern for problems of knowledge. If they are to work they have need of the insights of the historian, expressed clearly in ordinary language. This field in the United Kingdom has been given the name 'Intelligent Knowledge-Based Systems'. The computing world is short of experts in the intelligent handling of knowledge, and lacks much of the necessary underlying theory. Some historians have started collaborative research and teaching activities, and we can begin to identify possibilities and choose priorities for the future. It is important that we express the possibilities and priorities in terms of history rather than of computing at this stage. Computers and computing are undergoing revolutionary changes at present: the nature of history remains constant though the tools available for its pursuit may change.

For purposes of analysis I will identify three particular important areas of development:

Intelligent information retrieval.
Modelling and simulation.
Explanation and advice.

As will emerge, these areas are far from mutually exclusive. The Historical Association pamphlet *Computers in secondary school history teaching* discussed work in the first two areas, largely using examples from work with minicomputers. Computer technology is now much cheaper, more powerful, and more widely available, as well as being better able to deliver on some of the needs of the historian. There is increasing evidence to support Joseph Hunt's hope that "the great source of the computer in the classroom will be to involve the pupil, far more than hitherto, in active enquiry".

1.2 INTELLIGENT INFORMATION RETRIEVAL

Historians need to obtain and make sense of information, regarded as evidence in the context of a particular problem under examination. Collingwood placed great emphasis on the activity of asking questions, which he described as "the dominant factor in history, as it is in all scientific work". The historian reads his primary and secondary sources "with a question in his mind, having taken the initiative by deciding for himself what he wants to find out from them". Whereas Beverley Labbett has written of "squeezing" his evidence, Collingwood writes of "putting it to the torture, twisting a passage ostensibly about something quite different into an answer to the question he has decided to ask". The historian needs to be able to ask questions as and when he wants to, and not in a restricted manner laid down by someone else: "It is not enough to cover the ground by having a catalogue of all the questions that have to be asked, and asking every one of them sooner or later: they must be asked in the right order". Asking questions is not enough; one needs to be able to develop and test one's own hypotheses relative to the available evidence. This testing is itself carried out through questionning. "Every time the historian asks a question, he asks it because he thinks he can answer it; that is to say, he has already in his mind a preliminary and tentative idea of the evidence he will be able to use." At the end of the process of enquiry, Collingwood says, the historian hopes to place himself in a position where he can say "the facts which I am now observing are the facts from which I can infer the solution of my problem".

Compared with the sophistication that we require of a computer system to make it a useful extension of the research capacity of the historian or the teaching facilities in a history classroom, standard information retrieval packages available for school microcomputers have serious limitations. Current research in the field of computer science and artificial intelligence offers possibilities of considerable improvements.

(a) Query Systems

It is clearly unsatisfactory to limit the kind of question that can be asked, or to offer only a prespecified range. We need systems that allow the user to describe the information that he wants. Ideally he should be able to do this in English or another natural language. Such systems are being developed, where the computer program has a knowledge of the vocabulary of the particular subject area, and can translate the phrasing of the question into the terms in which the information is expressed in the database. A further step would be to allow spoken questions, recognized and understood by the computer system. Real natural language understanding is extremely complex, and will require larger computers than are currently available in schools.

(b) Databases and knowledge representation

The historian's potential need for the assistance of the computer is greater when he is dealing with a large volume of complex information of variable format. Joseph Hunt quoted the *Times Literary Supplement:* "The computer's demand for homogeneous material seems to have continually encountered the historian's sensitivity to the complex realities involved". There are notable cases, such as the work in Cambridge on the records of Earls Colne, where diverse records have been amalgamated for intelligent use, on large mainframe computers. Typically at school level, where an information retrieval package permits the addition of data chosen by the user, it has to conform to a particular form, and it is not usually possible to add generalization, rules, or related information to enrich the 'knowledge base' under examination. At the research level considerable work has been done on knowledge representation and acquisition, and sophisticated systems are becoming available that allow the user to develop his own complex database without technical expertise. There is of course then a burden on the historian to describe his information clearly and correctly.

There is considerable potential in the linking of different computers through intelligent networks. We could envisage, for instance, having a microcomputer in the classroom with a sophisticated query system linked to databases held on large mainframe computers in the same institution or at a distance. In certain cases we might link a microcomputer to a teletext system such as PRESTEL, or send a specific query to a library or museum by electronic mail. In each case the key component of the intelligent information system is the user, with his choice of question and information.

1.3 MODELLING AND SIMULATION

A number of historical computer simulations have been available for some years, but they tend to lack sophistication both in computing and, more importantly, in historical terms. Few historical programs have taken advantage of the range of graphics and sound facilities available on school and personal microcomputers: many have simply been translated from earlier minicomputer versions.

In historical terms I would be more critical. All too often a historical computer simulation could be carried out with pen and paper: there is a pre-set linear sequence of decisions to be made and a 'correct' answer to each question. 'Incorrect' responses receive little remedial attention, and the student does not have the opportunity to affect the learning experience. It tends to be impossible for the teacher to amend the program for his own purposes or to suit the needs of a particular class. The computer will provide complex information, in trading and business games in particular, but will not explain where it comes from. There will be an underlying model, formula, or program but this is not open to scrutiny or amendment.

A number of improvements can be made, and are being made, with improved understanding of the use of computer technology. The popular vogue for 'adventure games' can be turned to history teaching purposes, with an historical 'micro-world' created within which the individual can explore, making decisions that have clear consequences for the subsequent stages of the game. The sophistication of graphics and sound enhances the appeal of the material, but the historical content is important, and one needs to address the issue of classroom use: how many computers can we assume are to be available for such individual use? With greater memory facitilies becoming available we can add further sophistication, more alternative decisions (allowing 'branching' and not merely linear progress), and greater richness of information and description.

What, however, are we trying to simulate? The conventional simulation concerns the individual decision-maker, such as Drake or Lenin. We can also explore the relationships and decisions of groups of historical agents, each student playing a different role, supported by general and individual briefing materials relating to a particular situation. In order to take a sensible decision 'in character', the students have the aid of a database, available for questionning when needed. They can explore their own situation and that of others, review events to date, and add their own decisions. The focus of attention here is not the computer, but the classroom experience of participation by the students, supported by appropriate information. Two things are simulated: firstly the historical situation as brought to life by participating characters, and secondly the process of arriving at a historical account of the sequence of classroom events. In each case the computer can provide invaluable evidence in support.

A simulation exercise, then, can be concerned with recreating events from the point of view of the historical agents, and with describing events from the point of view of the historian. This assumes a degree of classroom activity, in particular discussion, that goes beyond the computer program. The computer is a catalyst, not a substitute, for classroom discussion.

The next step in this argument is to say that every history lesson should be a simulation. At the end of a lesson a student should have acquired greater understanding of history by having participated in the activity of being a historian. This does not imply an incessant flow of games. It does mean that teachers should look at the concepts that are being introduced, the chronological or other explanatory frameworks, the research techniques that are described, the archive sources mentioned as part of the work of the historian. Each can be modelled with the help of the computer.

Talk of models and modelling can cause disquiet, but it should be nothing new. We are accustomed to referring to the feudal system, to geographical and social mobility, to the cold war, to theories of Keynesian economics and monetarism, to deterrence and disarmament. We can remain secure with these abstractions, we who have lived and experienced something of their reality. Our students benefit from a concrete representation of such abstractions, something tangible and manipulable. Running a model as a program can render it comprehensible, more so if the model is open to scrutiny and amendment.

1.4 EXPLANATION AND ADVICE

Collingwood wrote "For history, the object to be discovered is not the mere event, but the thought expressed in it. To discover that thought is already to understand it. After the historian has ascertained the facts, there is no further process of inquiring into their causes. When he knows what happened, he already knows why it happened." The historian arrives at the facts following an interaction with the evidence. The techniques of that interaction must be learned.

For Collingwood, rules are at the heart of understanding and explanation: "The first question which any intelligent man asks, when he finds himself in a situation of any kind, is 'what are the rules for acting in this kind of situation?' " We should be able to assume a certain continuity, a regularity in a certain kind of case: "If you want to know why a certain kind of thing happened in a certain kind of case, you must begin by asking 'what did you expect?'. You must consider what the normal development is in cases of that kind. Only then, if the thing that happened in this case was exceptional, should you try to explain it by appeal to exceptional conditions".

Understanding and explanation are closely linked. When a computer, or a historian, gives a conclusion, one should be able to ask 'How did you arrive at that conclusion?' or 'Why did you not arrive at this alternative?', and an explanation should be available. Historians tire, and books are not open to this kind of interrogation. With the computer an account can be explored and tested. We should note that the question 'Why did you arrive at that conclusion?' is different, and may take into account facts about the historian (or computer) apart from the historical evidence itself.

Historians cannot be expected to know all the answers. They should have acquired the skill of asking the necessary questions. There may be particular questions that should be asked in a given situation, certain checks to be made on specific sources, customs to be understood in alien cultures or institutions. Such expertise can be made more widely available, not just through academic tomes published close to the retirement of the authors, but in programs that are accessible to teachers and students of history, known as expert systems.

There is a broader context for the consideration of the problem of explanation. Historians seek a coherent account of complex events. They are not so much concerned with causation in the scientific sense as with the reasons for human actions. These reasons are often clear with a fuller description of the facts. Collingwood drew the parallel with the problem for the jury trying a murder case, the case of John Doe. Whereas "a jury has to content itself with something less than scientific (historical) proof, namely with that degree of assurance or belief which would satisfy it in any of the practical affairs of daily life", for the historian the standards are higher. "Nothing matters to him except that his decision, when he reaches it, shall be right: which means, for him, that is shall follow inevitably from the evidence". Having arrived at the conclusion it can be explained in terms of the evidence.

Our three areas of development can all be regarded as falling in the domain of work in artificial intelligence (AI). O'Shea & Self in their book *Learning and teaching with computers* explain what artificial intelligence programs involve:

"remembering and accessing relevant knowledge;
using this knowledge appropriately, for example, to
    reason and to form plans of action;
revising and extending their knowledge;
searching in some more or less systematic way for a solution to a
    problem;
recognizing similarities and drawing analogies between things; and
attempting to understand some aspect of their surroundings,
    for example, something communicated to them in English"

The early years of artificial intelligence research were spent, largely in the United States, with expensive equipment and little contact with the classroom, though interesting work was done, particularly in simulation games and intelligent tutoring systems. In the last three years the languages LOGO and PROLOG have become generally available on microcomputers, and the same should soon be true of SMALLTALK.

micro-PROLOG has been used by history teachers in the United Kingdom, United States, France, and Australia. Using the small microcomputers generally available in schools, teachers have been addressing the three problem areas, working in collaboration with computer science specialists. Work to date has been reported by Ennals and Nichol, but the surface of the field has barely been scratched. British history teachers have an international reputation for innovative ideas — as evidenced by the overseas success of the Schools Council History 13—16 Project and of *Teaching History*. They are sometimes more hesitant than, in particular, their Australian colleagues in giving practical realization to their ideas.

There are considerable possibilities in this area. Work in artificial intelligence has achieved a new prominence in the United Kingdom since the Japanese Fifth Generation Computer Initiative and the Alvey Report on Advanced Information Technology. A recent Social Science Research Council report has emphasized the importance of an artificial intelligence approach to education. Government has provided support for a first generation of microcomputer hardware in our schools. micro-PROLOG and other artificial intelligence software is becoming available on the whole range of school microcomputers. The field is open for historians and teachers to explore the issues.

The future of the use of the computer in the study and teaching of history is in the hands of historians. Computer hardware is available, as is the software from which useful materials can be developed, together with some programs already produced. The need is for historians to become involved, to describe the information with which they are concerned and the way in which they wish to be able to interact with it. This implicitly involves a process of reflection on the nature of our subject and on the way in which we wish to approach it in the classroom. In explaining such things to a computer or a computer scientist we can come to a clearer understanding. This should not be surprising. The purpose of work in artificial intelligence is to extend our power of thinking and under-standing. It is a bonus to have in addition a program which can help the thinking and understanding of others. Furthermore, there is an argument that work in artificial intelligence, or in 'Intelligent Knowledge Based Systems' has need of the insights of historians. As Collingwood wrote: "the right way of investigating mind is by the methods of history". Alternatively, to misquote President Kennedy, "Ask not what the computer can do for you, but what you can do for the computer".

An earlier version of this chapter was given as an address to a conference of the Historical Association on "The use of the computer in the study and teaching of history" in February 1984. It was also reprinted in *Education, Telematique, Informatique* No. 1, Feb. 1984, published by Laboratoire d'Informatique pour les Sciences de l'Homme, LISH—CNRS Paris.

2

Making sense of the world

2.1 REVIEW OF THE LITERATURE

A major concern of mankind since the earliest societies has been to 'make sense of the world', to establish the limits of human activity, and to gain a greater understanding of human behaviour and reationality. A number of writers have located AI work in the tradition of the human sciences rather than the natural sciences. Here we attempt to broaden that analysis, identifying particular traditions which may benefit from incorporating the ideas and techniques of artificial intelligence.

Margaret Boden

Margaret Boden wrote in her *Artificial intelligence and natural man* (Boden, 1977)

> "Artificial Intelligence. . . has a potential for counteracting the dehumanizing influence of natural science, for suggesting solutions to many traditional problems in the philosophy of mind, and for illuminating the hidden complexities of human thinking and personal psychology"

and her account drew particularly on work in the fields of language, literature, philosophy, and psychology.

Herbert Simon

Herbert Simon drew on his own background in organization theory and economics in his early work in artificial intelligence research, and developed a synthesis of these different traditions in his *The sciences of the artificial* (Simon, 1969). Phenomena are described as artificial in a very specific sense: they are as they are only because of a system being moulded, by goals or purposes, to the environment. The natural sciences are concerned with the discovery of a partially concealed pattern behind observed complexity, whereas the artificial sciences are concerned with synthesis. They set out to imitate the appearance of natural things while lacking their reality. The underlying basis of these sciences of human behaviour is rationality. We are often able to predict behaviour from a knowledge of a system's goals and its outer environment.

In his work in economics Simon became aware of the power of simulation as a source of new knowledge. Working models, such as Phillips' Moniac at the London School of Economics, a hydraulic model of the Keynesian economy (Phillips, 1950), can make a complex problem more tractable. The operation of abstraction is seen as of central importance

"The more we are willing to abstract from the detail of a set of phenomena, the easier it becomes to simulate the phenomena. Moreover, we do not have to know, or guess at, all the internal structure of the system but only that part of it that is crucial to the abstraction."

In this context the computer has an obvious appeal

"The computer becomes an obvious device for exploring the consequences of alternative organizational assumptions for human behaviour."

Computers have enabled him to deal with ideas as he was accustomed to dealing with administrative structures:

"Computers have transported symbol systems from the platonic heaven of ideas to the empirical world of actual processes carried out by machines or brains, or by the two of them working together."

His focus on human problem-solving involves the breaking down of conventional barriers between subject areas:

"The real subject of the new intellectual free trade among the many cultures are our own thought processes, our processes of judging, deciding, choosing and creating. We are importing and exporting from one intellectual discipline to another ideas about how a socially organized information-processing system like a human being — or a computer, or a complex of men and women and computers in organized cooperation — solves problems and achieves goals in outer environments of great complexity."

R. G. Collingwood

There is considerable potential for further interaction between workers in artificial intelligence and those in history and the social sciences. R. G. Collingwood, in particular, worked as both a philosopher and a historian, and provides a rare fusion of theory and practical experience. (Collingwood 1939, 1946). His practical experience emphasized the need for theory:

"I had learnt by first-hand experience that history is not an affair of scissors and paste, but is much more like Bacon's idea of science. The historian has to decide exactly what it is that he wants to know; and if there is no authority to tell him, as in fact (one learns in time) there never is, he has to find a piece of land or something that has got the answer hidden in it, and get the answers out by fair means or foul."

He makes the unorthodox move of suggesting that history has a contribution to make to accounts of scientific method rather than the flow of assistance being all in the other direction. It is, he said

". . . a question of making good a defect in current theories of 'scientific' method by attending to an element in 'scientific' knowledge about which there seemed to be a conspiracy of silence, namely the historical element"

For him, history was the key to the investigation of 'mind':

"The right way of investigating mind is by the methods of history."

His account of historical knowledge is in terms of throught:

"Historical knowledge is the reenactment in the historian's mind of the thought whose history he is studying".
"Since history proper is the history of thought, there are no mere 'events' in history: what is miscalled an 'event' is really an action, and expresses some thought (intention, purpose) of its agent; the historian's business is therefore to identify this thought."

He distinguishes the meaning of historical and typical scientific questions with two examples:

"When a scientist asks, 'Why did that piece of litmus paper turn pink?' he means 'On what kind of occasions do pieces of litmus paper turn pink?'
When an historian asks 'Why did Brutus stab Caesar?' he means 'What did Brutus think, which made him stab Caesar?' "

Explanation is in terms of reasons for action, and for the historian scientific accounts of causation have little place.

Collingwood takes a radical approach to evidence in history, presenting it in terms of the process of asking historical questions. True history, he says, is:

"The practice of an autonomous kind of inferential thinking concerned not with testimony but with evidence: and evidence is defined not by the fact that it is received, or even by the fact that it is received and withstands critical examination, but by its relevance to the process of asking and answering historical questions."

On his view the meaning of an historical statement is a function of the question to which it is an answer. A right answer is one that "enables us to get ahead with the process of questionning and answering." Each question arises from the presuppositions formed from the answers to past questions. Each course of inquiry ends in absolute presuppositions, a system of concepts providing a formal structure for experience. Using this notion of absolute presuppositions, an historian can set up concepts and 'run' them without necessarily believing them to be true.

Problems are raised for the philosophy of history and its links with artificial intelligence by Collingwood's work. We seem obliged to forsake the causal explanations of science in order to give explanations in terms of reasons for action as Collingwood advocates.

Donald Davidson

Donald Davidson seeks to resolve this problem of explanation by developing the idea of rationalization. On his account a reason explains an action by giving the agent's reason for doing what he did. This is presented as a species of ordinary causal explanation. He expands the idea of rationalization as follows:

> "A reason rationalizes an action only if it leads us to see something the agent saw, or thought he saw, in his action — some feature, consequence or aspect of the action the agent wanted, desired, prized, held dear, thought dutiful, beneficial, obligatory or agreeable."

He argues that for us to understand how a reason of any kind rationalizes an action it is necessary and sufficient that we see, at least in essential outline, how to construct a primary reason. The primary reason for an action is presented as its cause:

> "R is a primary reason why an agent performed the action A under the description d only if R consists of a pro attitude of the agent towards actions with a certain property, and a belief of the agent that A, under the description d, has that property."

Interestingly, Davidson lays great emphasis on description, saying that the straight description of an intended result often explains an action better than stating that the result was intended or desired. The redescription of an action afforded by a reason may place the action in a wider social, economic, linguistic, or evaluative context. The two approaches of redescription and causal explanation are presented as compatible:

> "To describe an event in terms of its cause is not to identify the event with its cause, nor does explanation by redescription exclude causal explanation."

These issues should be seen in the context of debates on causation and explanation since the time of David Hume, which has involved participants such as Alan Robinson, and Tom Richards, now actively involved in work in computer science and artificial intelligence.

There is further considerable scope for cross-fertilization between the fields of structuralist social science and artificial intelligence. Our analysis here will draw on the work of Levi-Strauss, Foucault and Piaget.

Claude Levi-Strauss

Claude Levi-Strauss was a scholar and intellectual whose reputation in the Anglo-Saxon tradition of philosophy and social science has been unsure. Whereas recent researchers in his primary field of social anthropology have emphasized the importance of practical field research, his ultimate concern was different: to establish facts which were true about 'the human mind', rather than about the organization of any particular society or class of societies. Our emphasis should be on his method, rather than on the particular practical consequences of the use to which it has been put. In his work on kinship theory, the logic of myth, and the theory of primitive classification, Levi-Strauss was using his background of training in philosophy and law to develop the case for structuralism. Edmund Leach (Leach, 1970) has summarized the structuralist case:

> "When, as men, we construct artificial things (artifacts of all kinds), or device ceremonials, or write histories of the past, we imitate our apprehension of Nature: the products of our culture are segmented and ordered in the same way as we suppose the products of Nature to be segmented and ordered."

Leach controversially establishes a common tradition within which both structuralist theory and modern computer technology can be located, with founding figures such as Lewis Carroll, with his alter ego as mathematician and logician Charles Dodgson. Leach focuses on our new use of technology as a helpful tool for understanding early societies:

> "Primitive thought differs from scientific thought much as the use of an abacus differs from mental arithmetic, but the fact that, in our present age, we are coming to depend on things outside ourselves — such as computers — to help us with our problems of communication and calculation makes this an appropriate moment to examine the way that primitive people likewise are able to make sense of the events of daily life by reference to codes composed of things outside themselves — such as attributes of animal species."

On this account thinking can be regarded as consisting of the manipulations of reduced models of ideas which started out in the first place as words, which symbolize events' and 'things' in the environment external to the thinker. Such an account could also be given of computer programs. Leach would argue that in a sense man has gone full circle. Primitive man used things as instruments, and we are now in a position to design machines which can do a great deal of the manipulation on their own account, handling greater complexity and more levels of abstraction than can be accommodated in the brain of the thinker.

The attention given to myth by structuralist social scientists can be explained in the context of logic and thinking. Levi-Strauss wrote in *Structural anthropology* (Levi-Strauss, 1963):

> "The purpose of myth is to provide a logical model capable of overcoming a contradiction (an impossible achievement, if, as it happens, the contradiction is real)."

The central social structure with which social anthropologists have been concerned is the family, the subject of Levi-Strauss' influential work *The elementary structures of kinship* (Levi-Strauss, 1969). Elementary structures of kinship are described as:

"those systems in which the nomenclature permits the immediate deter-
mination of the circle of kin and that of affines, that is, those systems
which prescribe marriage with a certain type of relative, or alternatively,
those which, whilst defining all members of society as relatives, devided
them into two categories, viz possible spouses and prohibited spouses . . .
. . . Marriage rules, nomenclature and the system of rights and prohibitions
are indissociable aspects of one the the same reality, viz the structure of the
system under consideration."

The problems of such an analytical approach are manageable when the group
under consideration is small and relatively closed, when rules are explicit or
established through deductive inferences; but, when the size and fluidity of the
group increases, and its limits become imprecise, the program becomes singularly
complicated. At this stage, Levi-Strauss sees

". . tremendous difficulties which are the province, not of the social antro-
pologist, but of the mathematician."

Levi-Strauss draws the significant analogy with games, already a subject of
considerable research attention in artifical intelligence:

". . . the combinative possibilities of Crow-Omaha kinship systems also
suggest such complicated games as cards, draughts, and chess in which the
possible combinations, although theoretically finite, are so large in number
that, for all useful purposes and on the human scale, they might as well be
infinite."

Jean Piaget

The work of Piaget should be seen in the context of structuralism. Starting from
doctoral work in the classification of molluscs, he drew on the theoretical
mathematical structures of the Bourbaki group of French mathematicians to
represent the sequence of logical operations required for understanding and
manipulating complex knowledge areas. He was concerned with exploring the
way in which this sequence of logical operations was reflected in the stages of
cognitive development of children. At this stage no previous attempts had been
made to examine the thought of the child from the point of view of mathematical
logic. The task of the logician, said Piaget, was to formalize the structures
appropriate to the successive stages of development of the child's "coming to
terms with the real world." In his later work, such as *Psychology and epistemology* (Piaget, 1970) and *Structuralism* (Piaget, 1971) he was endeavouring to
link psychology, logic, and epistemology, and to present a structural account
of knowledge and understanding that explicitly relates to the work of Levi-Strauss,
Foucault, and Parsons. This is not the light in which his work is conventionally
regarded, and there remains enormous potential for the further development of
his theories by artificial intelligence researchers.

Michel Foucault

Michel Foucault has written widely on the history and philosophy of science, but little account has been taken of his work in Britain until recent years when translations from the orginal French have been more readily available. His history of insanity *Madness and civilisation* and his history of institutional medicine *The birth of the clinic* have been influential in their own right, but themselves reflect the philosphical and epistemological viewpoint put forward in *The order of things* and *The archaeology of knowledge.*

Foucault's starting point, in *The order of things,* is:

> "What if empirical knowledge, at a given time and in a given culture, did possess a well-defined regularity?"

He said that he

> "tried to explore scientific discourse not from the point of view of the individuals who are speaking, nor from the point of view of the formal structures of what they are saying, but from the point of view of the rules that come into play in the very existence of such discourse."

This has involved him in the monumental task of developing a new theory of knowledge, drawing on what he calls the "Archaeology of knowledge". His aim was to discover

> ". . . in what way. . . our culture has made manifest the existence of order, and how, to the modalities of that order, the exchanges owed their laws, the living beings their constants, the words their sequence and their representative value; what modalities of order have been recognized, posited, linked with space and time, in order to create the positive basis of knowledge as we find it employed in grammar and philology, in natural history and biology, in the study of wealth and politcal economy."

Foucault's basic unit of analysis is the statement, used for logical analysis, grammatical analysis, and analysis of speech-acts. Groups of statements are organized in discourses, which have their own histories of limits, divisions, transformations, and modes of dealing with time. These discourses are managed in knowledge systems which he calls 'archives', which govern what can be said. and how. An archive operates at a meta-level and

> "differentiates discourses in their multiple existence and specifies them in their own duration."

Peter Laslett

Many of the themes identified above have been explored by British academics, particularly in Cambridge, who have been concerned with the merging of the different disciplines in the human sciences. Peter Laslett has for a generation been a major influence on the philosophy and practice of history and the social sciences. He was co-editor of the four volumes of essays *Philosophy, politics and society* a series which sought to recreate an approach to social and political philosophy, and to the philosophy of history, and founder of the Cambridge Group for the History of Population and Social Structure. He has developed a particular interest in 'sociological history' or 'social structural history', taking ourselves as the starting point, and encouraging

> "the frank acceptance of the truth that all historical knowledge, from one point of view, and that an important and legitimate one, is knowledge about ourselves, and the insistence on understanding by contrast."

Conventional history appears to have avoided crucial issues of theory and method:

> "History has been written as if questions about social structure and types of society, questions about causation too, were fairly straightforward and answerable by common sense and a little economics."

He advocates a historical method based on reconstruction:

> "The imaginative reconstruction of a former society can only foster an interest in its people as people."

Laslett and his colleagues have made great use of quantitative methods in their research, and this has often worried more conventional historians. Laslett points out that historical work is inherently quantitative in an important sense:

> "Whenever a statement is made about a plurality of persons and it is claimed that they are more this than that, or mostly the one and not the other, on average like this rather than like anything else; whenever a propostion is made in social terms, whether it is about votes, or prices, or length of life, or the number of heirs likely to live long enough to succeed, or even about the distribution of opinions, or preferences, or beliefs, then quantities are in question."

There are of course dangers in quantitative analysis of lists of items, or entries in official records, in that the composers of such lists or entries were unaware of the final uses to be made of their work. Laslett in his introduction to Wrigley's *Introduction to English historical demography,* paints a picture of the educated priest or literate parish clerk scrawling the entry in the appointed book "with the puzzled faces of the illiterate peasants crowding round him."

> "Whether or not a sense of duty in the mind of a priest, duty to his order or duty to his flock, was sufficient to keep him at his task of registration consistently enough to earn our praise so long after he is dead, it is impossible to imagine that he could ever have anticipated being judged on our criteria."

As one who has himself bridged several disciplines during his career, he is a strong advocate of historians taking advantage of insights and methods offered by the social sciences, philosophy, and mathematics:

> "Throughout my life at the university, men have been calling for the merger of disciplines. Now that the moment is come, it is not for the historian to drawback: unless, of course, he really believes that others better qualified than himself can now do that job better than he can."

Given such an approach, he declared in *The world we have lost:*

> "History, I believe, is about to claim a new and more important place in the sum total of human knowledge."

In recent years the work of the group has made increasing use of computer technology, as in the work on the records of Earls Colne 1350–1750 directed by Alan Macfarlane, a historian and social anthropologist.

Anthony Giddens

Another Cambridge scholar, Anthony Giddens, has tried to link the disciplines. He has written prolifically in the area of social theory, linking the traditions of history, sociology, and linguistic philosophy. Both Laslett and Giddens make frequent reference to the philosophical writings of Wittgenstein. As Giddens writes (Giddens, 1979):

> "I take the significance of Wittgenstein's writings for social theory to consist in the association of language with definite social practice. . . "

Giddens combines an analysis in terms of structures with a Wittgensteinian account of following rules in social life. He quotes Braudel (Braudel, 1969):

> "By structures, observers of the social mean an organization, coherence, relatively fixed relations between social realities and groups. For us historians, a structure is no doubt fabrication, architecture, but more than this a reality which time erodes only slowly."

In his theory of structuration, Giddens introduces the idea of conditions governing the continuity or transformation of structures over time. Laslett has had a similar concern for problems of time, finding notions like 'perdurance', continuance over time, of great help in describing and explaining changes in population and social structure. The investigation of phenomena such as population turnover has led to the massive disruption of conventional historical orthodoxy, as has the detailed analysis of documentary records of English and French villages.

French social historians

It should be noted at this stage that the Cambridge group of historians has been much influenced by the work and methods of French social historians of the Annales School. Many British historians have researched aspects of modern French social and political history (such as Cobb, Judt, Lyons, Hufton), and similar methods have been applied to modern British history, including some comparative demographic studies. The language barrier has meant that much excellent French work has had a limited audience. I have translated some examples of recent work, particularly from Marseilles, where historians and other human scientists have the assistance of a specialist computer laboratory. For them concepts of structure, and of social and political philosophy are alive and flourishing, in marked contrast to the relative aridity of British philosophy against which Laslett has struggled. As my translations indicate, they see a natural affinity between the problems of historians and the techniques of artificial intelligence and computer science.

2.2 TRANSLATIONS FROM FRENCH HUMAN SCIENTISTS

I am grateful to my colleagues at LISH (Laboratoire pour l'Informatique dans les sciences de l'homme) in Marseilles for their hospitality and for permission to translate some of their papers to give them a wider audience.

BORILLO, M.

A propos des bases de donnees: sur le role des sciences de l'homme dans le developpement de l'informatique

in: eds CHOURAQUI, E. & VIRBEL, J.
> *Banques d'informations dans les les sciences de l'homme*
> Monographies d'informatique de l'AFCET
> Editions Hommes et Technique 1981

translated by Richard Ennals as:
> 'Databases and the role of the human sciences in the development of computer science'

In the examination of the relationships between computer science and the human sciences, attention has until now been focused on the impact which computer science could not fail to have on research in the human sciences. This has not just been from the point of view of scientific results but also from the perspective of the organization of research, its economic management, the teaching of the human sciences, and indeed its applications.

I would now like to examine what is in a sense the reciprocal relationship: the effects on research in computer science which could arise from its encounter with the human sciences. I therefore address myself in the first instance to computer scientists. But it seems to me that this symmetrical approach is wholly necessary if we are to really understand the complexity of the new situations created by the encounter of some of the most advanced forms of technology and of scientific methodology with the disciplines which are, themselves, among the most ancient and important in the formation of our present culture.

It seems to me that this examination, in order to limit itself simply to issues concerning computer science research, must be broken down into four areas of a somewhat different nature. I will distinguish between

— the aspects of 'diffusion' — that is to say new areas of application opened up for computer science,
— useful aspects for computer science, which certain disciplines in the human sciences could bring to theoretical development and technical innovation,
— scientific aspects, from the perspective of theoretical and methodological suggestions which could be made by human scientists,

finally it would be a mistake to omit the humanist dimension, ethical references to which must be made by computer science through its dialogue with the human sciences, which go beyond strictly technical or economic issues which have to date circumscribed our account of social implications.

(1) *The human sciences as a new applications domain*

Of course the novelty we have mentioned should be regarded as relative, and computer science has for years played an important role in economics, in the management of public affairs, and also in the area of 'social control'.

The novelty, in our view, resides in the role devolved to computer science, and especially to its material and conceptual products such as databases, in the provision of tools for research in the human sciences. Under the same heading — but not under the same conditions — as happened thirty-five years ago with physics, chemistry, astronomy, and more recently biology. . .

I remain certain that the fundamental differences between natural sciences and human sciences are likely to bring computer science into the scientific scheme of things. I limit myself here to recollecting a few instances in terms of the 'market', to indicate what is happening in a crude manner through the imbalances caused by the weight of computation in the budgets of research teams in the human sciences. I also think of the increasingly frequent appearance of technicians or of computer science researchers among teams of sociologists, political scientists, linguists, anthropologists, historians. . .

Of course this extension of the 'market' for computer science does not reveal itself purely in financial terms and in terms of creating employment for computer scientists. More subtle effects can be detected, if not clearly seen: one could ask whether the alliance of the human sciences and computer science could be capable of opening up new outlets for the human sciences, which one imagines could bring a dowry of further possible applications areas: and whether this would not itself lead computer science into such new areas.

Perhaps one should also ask oneself, at the level of collective images, about aspects of symbolic legitimacy which computer science could eventually gain from its association with the human sciences, at a time when in certain countries the social image of computer science is extremely poor.

(2) *The human sciences as sources of knowledge and as a stimulus for new theoretical and methodological research*

Under this heading I will describe the more intrinsically scientific aspects of the contributions of the human sciences to the alliance. It is important, in the exploration of the complexity of these relationships, to distinguish two things: on the one hand the contribution of wisdom, knowledge, experience which the human sciences or at least certain of their disciplines can contribute to the development of this or that activity in computer science; and on the other hand, the incitements, the provocations to new research which the human sciences present to computer science in the form of new problems, questions not yet dealt with in the scientific tradition in which they are encountered.

I will start with this latter perspective, which seems to me to lead to more radical changes of direction, even though the two frameworks (which one could roughly characterize as: thematic contents of knowledge for the first, structure of knowledge for the second) are self-evidently inseparable.

From this point of view which consists of trying to discern the underlying abstractions of these kinds of influences, it is clear that the notions of data, of database, of systems for interrogating databases, and also the notion of a model or that of a procedure for testing hypotheses, can all be collected under the general heading of systems for representation and systems for manipulating representations, whatever may be their other formal characteristics, logical and semantic structure, properties of framework, at this fundamental level, where we find perhaps the most significant elements of the potential impact of the human sciences.

What I am saying is that there are essential fundamental differences between the phenomena and problems of the natural sciences — whose formalization has to a large extent flowed from the development of mathematics and thus through mathematics also from the development of computer science — and the phenomena and problems that comprise the substance of the human sciences.

Let us rather say, to make things clearer, that there is within the human sciences a part which, at least at the moment, is outside the research and methods of description and formalization which have been tried and tested in the natural sciences. For example, describing the contents of a text or giving a formal characterization of its style and ultimately the structure of the argument; the same operations, or at least the first two, can be applied to paintings; or again the objective analysis of such and such a pattern of behaviour in order to integrate it into a satisfactory theoretical context. . .

We can see that there is a long list of problems for which great numerical tables, however large they may be, with their limited structures and their constraints, are only really weak modes of representation. Such tables are reductionist in the real sense of the term, of complexities and details which we must be able to explain with pertinent facts, that is to say with representations in which the expert or the scholar can see the basis of his preoccupations.

Besides, although computer science started with the problems of physics and operational research which constituted its initial domain, in order to tackle problems of understanding text — which involves ambiguity and fulness of language — or problems of directing information systems — through which the complexities of social organization are also introduced — it has progressively developed tools appropriate for the representation of new phenomena and problems, which are not simply reducible to their equivalent in terms of natural science. Thus different modes have appeared, as we know, of historical databases, network models, relational models, object based relational models etc. . .

At the same time, for predominantly practical reasons, the idea has developed of separating the construction and the manipulation of such representations. The unforeseen productiveness of this idea itself is partly a product of actual research in procedural and assertional languages.

The direction of this evolution is pretty obvious, and it is even clearer when we consider current research in knowledge representation or expert systems which in a sense are the natural continuation of past work. In this field, the logical and semantic structures of the systems of representation in the chosen area and the inferential capacity which is associated show clearly that the explicit and implicit approaches of the researcher draw on the empirical model of natural language.

The formal systems which have been proposed — and they are becoming numerous — are all concerned, more or less, with reproducing through paraphrase some aspect or other of the expressive capacity of the infinite complexity of language.

We know that the role of language constituting discourse, argumentative or rhetorical — or more generally in reasoning — is fundamental in the development and description of knowledge in the human sciences. That is to say that the research in computer science to which I have referred is getting closer, without having intended it, to one of the most important focuses of attention in the human sciences: at the methodological level, how to capture and represent concepts and their articulation in a form of reasoning: or at a more fundamental level, the examination of the theoretical status of the formalisms constituting these representations. The structural control of descriptive systems is no less necessary in the area of databases; having defined the relational model with its expressive capacities, computer science asks the first-order logician to clarify its theoretical properties.

The time has come for computer science to take account of this profound theoretical convergence and to draw from it all appropriate potential benefits. Obviously in order to do this we must spend less time with cartoon-level problems concerning cats and mice and the problems of the customer in understanding a restaurant menu. . . , and regard as a probably more revealing intellectual area in scientific terms the way in which the historian or the archaeologist justifies certain of his inferences, or in which the sociologist introduces apparently paradoxical relational structures between his entities, or in which the lawyer uses analogies between conflicting situations that appear at first sight to have nothing in common.

In other words, the human sciences offer to computer science a collection of modes of reasoning which although they do not have the empirical characteristics — natural language and not formal systems — or the structural characteristics — natural logics and not formal classical deductive systems — of mathematics or theoretical physics, still have a certain coherence which computer science should progressively understand and characterize. This must happen if ambitions of automating intellectual operations are to be applied to the solution of real problems.

However, these problems are not merely logical, but also semantic and pragmatic. The notion of reasoning, in as much as it has been studied in a scientific tradition which forms part of the basis of our culture, united them in the multiplicity of their empirical and conceptual forms.

Today, current research in linguistics, cognitive psychology, the theory of rights and legal argument, analytical philosophy . . . offer a store of knowledge on which computer science is already drawing and which is serving to modify such fundamental notions as that of deduction and to enlarge the range of formal systems which can be unified or analysed.

Everthing indicates that theoretical research in the intelligent application of computer science is increasingly involved with research in modes of reasoning and, through that, formal research in the human science, research in which databases play a central role.

Having reached this point perhaps it is worth resuming the earlier distinction between the two frameworks of relationships between computer science and the human sciences: on the one hand, the structure of scientific discourse, as a sketch of certain logical–semantic models: on the other hand, the thematic contents of the discourse, the particular knowledge and skills that computer science could borrow. Recalling them briefly and associating with each recent technological developments, we could cit, for example:

– for oral communication man-machine: phonology, studies of prosody,
– for interactive computing: psychology, ergonomics,
– for word processing: linguistics of sentences and text.

It is not worth pursuing this further, as more examples can be added each day; to the extent that the technological development of computer science is increasingly integrated into the social fabric, and associated with an increasing range of human activities, it is clear that the effectiveness of this involvement and its results involve the assimilation of human and social knowledge of the context within which we are working.

It is on this point, which is likely to be one of the key issues for our immediate future, that I wish to end.

(3) *Computer sciences and human sciences: means or knowledge?*
Everything seems to have been said about the dangers of information technology for the individual and for society, and I will not dwell on that. My proposal is simply to suggest how the examination of the numerous subtle links between computer science and the human sciences can contribute to better understanding of what they can offer to computer science, or rather to computer scientists – the means of dealing with some of these dangers and of keeping, or regaining, a moral legitimacy that is currently in question.

It seems to me important to distinguish functional and cognitive outcomes. Just looking at the scale of the resources involved respectively in the areas of knowledge and of the economy, the reciprocal links of computer science and the human sciences have to date been particularly oriented to the perspective of production, of management of goods and of people.

One could think, and it is in any case a fundamental presupposition of our humanist tradition, that knowledge, the rational understanding of phenomena, by its very nature introduces into the technical and social game the elements which can enable us to keep in check and excessive blind proliferation of a technology that has become its own end.

The extension of research into computer methods in the human sciences, their progressive assimilation into standard methodologies of the varied disciplines, the theoretical advances which they are beginning to facilitate; there are numerous signs which bear testimony to the fact that the encounter of computer science and the human sciences could in future be regarded as an important moment for the emergence of knowledge about man and society whose increasing rigour in some ways guarantees its critical survival.

Isn't there something in this apparent sidetrack, in a somewhat surprising manner at first sight, which puts the case for computer science in the very area where it has most been under attack, in the name of the fundamental values of our civilization, fertile as well as at times superficial?

CHAMOUX A.
Family reconstitution: hopes and realities
Informatique et Histoire IRIA 1979

translated by Richard Ennals as:

Computers the order of the day — a state of mind .

Computers are now the order of the day in historical research. It is not the computer that has brought about this micracle, but the researcher himself. The growth of historical demography has led to the spread of methods of family reconstitution developed by Louis Henry in 1956 with parish records. We have now lost count of the number of monographs on village history which have come to enrich our knowledge of populations in the past. In certain countries it is possible to go back further than the seventeenth century. There has been a general immersion in civil state records, religious registers, poll books. In individual research and collective research it is still the case that the manual methods of family reconstitution, although now well known, cannot help the historian skilled in the craft to attack large units, that is to say towns.

Thus the attraction of the computer. Working on the history of Caen, J-C Perrot, in collaboration with a computer laboratory in Toulouse, succeeded in sorting family records on the computer, using a special program. He only dealt with one parish in the town. But his work was the first to be carried through to completion. Much bigger studies are currently being carried out. There is the case of Reims. Our experience with this large town under the Ancien Regime has allowed us to see clearly the problems relating to the use of the computer with historical data. . .

The problem in family reconstitution is recognizing the same person in different documents. The human brain is capable of recognizing and approximating. To accomplish such links with a machine we have to describe exactly what criteria are relevant, and organize them in a hierarchy. As parish registers have been poorly maintained and we rarely find information about jobs and ages at death, the linkage of documents is very difficult.

This is why Schofield's work has been so worthwhile, for the English records are particularly dificient in this respect. The operation of this program is so slow because it has to make such a series of calculations to choose between good and bad linkages generated by the machine. This is without taking into account the fact that in England the wife loses her maiden name on marriage, which further complicates the task of establishing parental links. Add to this the changes in the calendar. However, the English have the incomparable advantage over us of possessing for numerous parishes the complete records transcribed and published by genealogical societies. They are not content with this, and revert to the original text, but they have available a research tool for which we envy them.

CHOURAQUI, E. & VIRBEL, J.
Presentation *Banques d'informations dans les sciences de l'homme:*
in: eds Chouraqui, & Virbel
> Monographies d'informatique de l'AFCET
> Editons Hommes et Techniques 1981

translated by Richard Ennals as:

Data bases in the human sciences

The analysis and handling of information in the human sciences is without doubt as long established as most other human activities – remember, for example, that the interpretation of sacred or legal texts, or the keeping and use of lists and catalogues of all sorts, seem inseparable from the first known historical examples of writing – and has depended for a considerable time on diverse methods of reconstruction, organization, and archive management of data. Modern development of these techniques has concentrated enormous investments, both intellectual and technical, particularly since researchers in the human social sciences have taken to using information technology. At the present time these methods, currently expanding fast, are producing a vast expansion in the field of what it is convenient to call the informatization of society. However, such an activity, involving the combination of two spheres of research – information technology on the one hand and human sciences on the other hand – does not always have the organization and rigour that all scientific activities of this nature must have. If the relative weakness of the forms of the methods developed in the sphere of the humanities and social sciences is at the root of this combination of fields, it should not remain so for long as it was essentially due to the vast variety of situations encompassed by the two fields, which have also tended to increase in complexity with the development of methodology and particular techniques.

In fact the human and social sciences, to start with them, reflect already a vast spread of disciplines, which interdisciplinary activity tends to modify and overlap further among themselves. These disciplines are based on the study of a wide range of problems, where reference to the fundamental elements constituting scientific research, necessary for productive interaction with the world of computer science (definition of data, agreement on descriptions, explicit statement of operations of manipulation and reasoning of sets of data, etc) tends to be unstable, varying from one case to another. Furthermore, the very nature of the data ('artifacts', texts, archives, biographies, pictures, behaviour, spatial organisation) and its means of analysis and processing (statistical, linguistic, mathematical, logical, etc.) is also extremely diversified, and presents methodological problems in analysis and representation which vary considerably between cases. Finally, and perhaps most importantly, familiarity with computer science techniques is extremely variable according to disciplines, problems, organizations, and traditions of work, varying from massive general use to timid stabs at fringe research.

Computer science or information technology, for its part, particularly as 'the science of information and its communication', covers a vast spectrum of questions of a different nature but a comparable variety, among which certain are independent of the nature of particular applications, and others are very directly connected to them. Computer science involves a complex overlapping of levels of reality, going from the purely instrumental (computers with their physical properties: size, speed, architecture, etc.) to the formalisms lying at the foundations of research in their use. The machine cannot be put to use without an environment, itself made up of component parts, including peripheral equipment (devices for data capture and output etc.) and means of communication at different levels (development systems, specific programs, etc.).

As for the formal basis of computer science, it covers a variety of methods (linguistic, statistical, logical, combinatorial, etc.) which lie at the basis of different languages for data representation, processing, and programming, etc.

Moreover, these two fields are not static. Human sciences, or at least certainly the component disciplines, are creating new paradigms; interdisciplinary research suggests new fields of investigation; new methods are defined, including as well new questions to be asked, or new research methods for tackling classical questions, new documents not previously taken into account and from which it is possible to form new data. As for the differences and changes in computer science, at the present time these consist of changes at the instrumental or equipment level (telecommunications, microprocessors, dedicated machines etc.) as well as at the level of formalisms (development of nonclassical logics, complex systems of knowledge representation and reasoning, extremely advanced programming languages, etc.).

Computer-aided information processing – from its simple use indicating the functional character of the objectives being pursued to the solving of particular problems formulated with its help and indicating the cognitive character of objectives to be achieved – cannot be carried out until an organized collection of operations has been previously performed: the collection of the raw materials comprising the information to be processed, the analysis of these materials in a manner functionally related to the kind of processing to be performed, the extraction and representation of relevant information, and finally the design and implementation of the database containing this information. We can recognize there the principal stages of database construction which are themselves at present undergoing changes. Databases are one of the elements comprising information systems: the other being represented by the combination of administrators and users of these databases. The implementing of such systems in the first place poses institutional problems by the very fact of their insertion into the systems for transfer of information. The effectiveness and the duration of any enterprise of this nature depends naturally on the manner in which these problems are resolved; some simple questions lie at the roots. Who should take the intitiative in the creation of a database of information in this or that sector of the human sciences? An individual researcher, a laboratory, a specialist organization, etc? What should be the objectives? Technological, documentary, scientific, etc? For what kinds of users? Researchers, practitioners, the general public, etc? Should these information systems be regional, national (in one language) or international (in many languages)? Who should build the infrastructure capable of taking on these different tasks? An adminstrative service, a multidisciplinary team of researchers, and/or technicians etc? All these questions, and many more as well, are raised, and the answers must contribute to the introduction of much more coordination and continuity in the process of implementing databases in the human sciences.

However, the scientific and technical problems posed by the theory and implementation of these knowledge bases or databases are just as fundamental. They do not merely concern the methodological aspects of analysis and representation of knowledge areas subjected to investigation, but also the formal and technical aspects of representation and processing of data. This problem area is evolving, thanks to the continual progress of research in this area of activities which is essentially multidisciplinary, and which thus draws on numerous disciplines such as computer science, logic, linguistics, etc. Technical and economic developments consequent on the results of this research progressively change institutional choices and decisions – which by this very fact are beyond the level of individual technicians – and thus play a central role in the creation and administration of information systems.

GUENOCHE, A. & HESNARD, A.
Typologie d'amphores Romaines par une methode logique de classification
LISH Marseille November 1982
Revue: Computer and the Humanities

translated by Richard Ennals as:

Typology of Roman Amphora

Research into the classification of collections of facts or of objects is central to the human sciences; it is part of the organization of an area of knowledge, and produces a better understanding of the knowledge being classified. This is why in recent years there has been so much interest among statisticians and mathematicians who have proposed purely formal methods for producing automatic classifications whose justification consists entirely in the description given to the objects, their measurements, and an algorithm. But this view of the problem, which is becoming increasingly well defined in mathematical terms, is still far from the views of human scientists on classification and what he expects from such research.

Let us examine this idea more closely with reference to an apparently limited archaeological example with is, as we shall see, representative of the way in which the problem of classification is often encountered in the human sciences: we have been studying a type of Roman amphora commonly known as 'Dressel 2–4'. Rather than proposing a theoretical analysis and solution of an abstract nature which would add to those already avaiable, we will expound our method in analysing a real problem of classification which has not been resolved by tranditional archaeological methods. We emphasize at each step the more general applications of this particular example.

Amphora of the type Dressel 2–4; problem areas

We are concerned with large pottery wine containers used for the commercial distribution of wine in the Roman Empire between the middle of the first century BC and the end of the first century AD. They are generally known as 'Dressel 2–4 amphoras' after the work of H. Dressel who published the printed inscriptions carried on this kind of amphora, found in Rome.

The origin of this problem of classifying the amphoras was the publication of these Roman painted inscriptions. The names of the wines carried in the Dressel 2–4 amphora can be traced to a wide range of different areas of production: Campania, Etruria, Narbonne, Tarragon, and probably many others. None of the amphora forms 2–4 corresponding to one source and one alone. They can in fact be grouped according to a number of criteria:

— a resemblance to the wood cut designs in the collection of Latin inscriptions which, even if it is not always explicit, bears a stronger resemblance to them than to all other amphora
— painted inscriptions which clearly related to amphoras of wine at the same period, containing the same wine.

But, at the same time, neither classification is wholly satisfactory:

— from the point of view of form: although we know roughly the differences that distinguish them from other amphoras, we are still puzzled by the infinite variety to be found within the group, which also explains the wide range of vocabulary used to describe them in the archaeological literature
— the wines indicated come from different areas: there was no common source.

We are left, as F. Zevi has remarked, with 'a confusing and unsatisfactory picture'. This is how he describes the contradiction between the impression of a certain unity in the forms as in the destination of the objects, and, at the same time, the impression of internal diversity indicated by the inscriptions but which fails to correspond to the 'variants of forms' or sub-groups indicated by H. Dressel: forms 2, 3, 4, and 5.

Forms 2–4 of the Dressel Amphora are a 'family' of amphora with similar morphology, without there being a formal definition of the form, which seems to obtain between amphora of the first century, without us being able to ascribe a common origin. In fact, we would state that normally we group together objects that are pretty much the same under a common name, with variations according to the observer, and we are putting forward the hypothesis that the same is true in the case of wine amphoras.

A negative confirmation of this view is provided by the reasons given for excluding Dressel 5 amphoras from this group:

— their morphological characteristics
— their inscriptions, in Greek, which give no names of the wines.

We are therefore dealing with what in archaeological terms is considered a recognized grouping of amphoras, and with a choice of possible regions of origin. A large amount of extrinsic information is available from a small number of objects. This information is of a miscellaneous nature and could involve:

— the archaeological context of discovery, which could be a source of information (workshop, wrecked ship, etc.)
— graphic information carried on certain objects, a painted inscription giving for instance the name of a vineyard, known from other sources and capable of being located and assigned a date
— information concerning the clay mixture with which the object was made, or perhaps visual observations of distinguishing characteristics of certain geographical zones – for example the volcanic clay of the Vesuvius region – or chemical analysis which allows us to associate the objects with particular workshops.

We must remember that extrinsic data regarding origin are only available in very few cases, about a hundred; for all the others, which can be numbered in thousands, where we do not know the source of origin, the only data available are intrinsic, morphological. Given the objective of developing a typology whose role is to analyse different forms – thus intrinsic data – according to sources evidenced by extrinsic data, we must try to apply to the analysis of all Dressel 2–4 amphoras the knowledge that we have on a few of them.

This step allows us to use the amphora as evidence for the wines which they contained: it is thus crucial to studies of commerce and trade at the time. We must therefore develop a hypothesis that the published taxonomy, which is supported by the extrinsic data, can be used as evidence with the aid of anthropological data, or, in other words, that different winemaking regions had different forms of amphora, which obliges us to use as a premise the typological construction that two amphoras with identical inscriptions come from the same source.

We are here considering a common situation in the human sciences: the problem of establishing a typology according to a partially known list of categories, with the help of descriptive variables which we seek to associate with those categories, although there is no *a priori* evidence to support their association.

The typology

Classically, an automatic system of classification operates on a collection of objects that have no *a priori* structure and are described by a choice of descriptive variables. We use the word choice deliberately because all description is an interpretation, an implicit decision, to only take a particular view of an object. An archaeologist must often give a full justification for this choice: in the best cases he can explain his motivations and the semantic family of descriptions used (concerning physical dimensions, those with unusual characteristics through their precious metal contents, etc.). This is why the majority of classification algorithms tend to miss the point of the problem of weighing variables — how much importance they should be given, whether they should be suppressed, and particularly how to synthesize the relevant descriptive details in the expression of a coefficient of resemblance or difference between objects, whose consistent application will enable us to quantify the similarities between any pairs of objects. Indeed these methods in themselves are not concerned with the problem of data itself, but solely with defining means of combination and quantification — methods of ascending hierarchies or dynamic connections, or of separation, dichotemous methods for arriving at a classification, or a classification tree.

The foregoing analysis must lead us to reassess the formal approach if we do not discard it entirely. It is no longer a question of finding a weighting of descriptive variables, a scale in this space of variables (to quantify resemblances), and an algorithm with which to confirm the sources of these objects where they are known; this means of proceeding is surely doomed to failure.

A small amount of practical experience of classification in no matter what domain leads one to pose the question 'Why this form of classification?' and to return to the logic of the algorithm (if the quantity of data makes this possible). One can see that it is in the characterization of objects and in the definition of their points of resemblance, modelled using the chosen scaling factors, that one can find the 'reason' behind the algorithm and its products. So, to the extent that one expects a significant result, it is only a question of modifying the premises, description, and scale so that, an unlikely outcome, we can obtain a sensible classification.

This is why we prefer the approach which consists in finding a morphological common feature in a collection of objects whose source is known, extending the same source to other objects with the same common feature, under the heading of a hypothesis, of comparing their extrinsic characteristics with this hypothesis of source, of considering it as acceptable or of rejecting it and then finding another morphological common feature. This approach is applied to each known source region. It allows us to collect together, in a functional manner, items incontestably from some embryonic group which, moreover, is defined by the common morphological characteristics. This approach does not classify all objects *a priori,* and conforms with the idea that perhaps we do not know all the sources, and thus the certain objects belong to none of the chosen groups of sources of origin.

We are therefore in a theoretical situation which has been described by J. C. Gardin as 'logico-empirical classification', whose principles are:

— to not separate the objects from their archaeological context, that is to say to take account of extrinsic data in depending on them to construct the typology
— to integrate the classification stage into archaeological research, making the reasoning explicit
— to try to establish a classification which relates to the objective for which it was assigned.

This approach is not specific to this particular problem, but applies to the human sciences in general where research in classification plays a part — if it doesn't, then there is no problem anyway — which must be integrated into the account of the particular research domain, otherwise one will certainly find oneself with an uninterpretable result and/or where one already has some embryonic classification, with the uncertainty as to the classification of certain objects. It is on this basis that we have built our approach.

The validation of the approach is assured by its formal coherence and most of all by the force of the interpretation of the problem and the data expressed by the final typology.

HENIN, Beatrice
Les loyers Marseillais du XVIIeme siecle avec le logiciel MICROBASE
HMCI numero 2 IHMC/LISH CNRS June 1983

translated by Richard Ennals as:

Seventeenth century leasehold agreements in Marseilles

Legal lease agreements for Marseilles in the seventeenth century are in the form of contracts stipulating the name and profession of the landlord and of his tenant, the nature of the accommodation rented, its location, the length of the lease, and the methods of payment. I was led to handle these documents in a quantitative manner and to use a microcomputer in my research on practical aspects of living conditions in Marselles in the seventeenth century.

The origins of this research were determined by an unprecedented event in the history of our town: an order for expansion given by Louis XIV in 1666. This was a far-reaching urban extension through which it was planned to treble the area of the town. This was a response by its promoter — the King, and then his representative in Marseilles, Arnoul, the supervisor of the floating prisons — to three kinds of necessity. The political necessities first of all. They had to stamp the impression of royal power in the soil of a city with a tradition of rebellion, and, to this end, they proceeded to build a citadel, a fort, and an arsenal and to destroy the ramparts. Next, the economic necessities. We must bear in mind the economic value of this remarkable natural seaport of Marseilles. It exceeded that of Brest, Lorient, and Rochefort which were built at the same period. Finally, sociological necessity. They needed to create new quarters with wide roads and enormous houses where the aristocracy, the landowning bourgeoisie, and royal officials could move after abandoning the old town, its winding narrow streets, and its cramped houses, to the ordinary people.

My problem derived from this last source: it consisted in finding out where there was an evolution in living conditions in Marseilles occasioned by this operation of extension, that is to say, an evolution in the variety of houses, their modes of occupation, the price of rented accommodation, and in the social make-up of each quarter.

The procedure adopted was the following: in the first place, it was a question of deciding on a chronological period for study. Rather than attempting to cover the whole century, it appeared preferable to concentrate attention on two periods: the first before the extensions (1610–1630), the other immediately afterwards (1666–1690). It was next necessary to determine a geographical area of study. Marseilles was then made up of four quarters. Two of these were particularly significant: Saint–Jean and Le Corps de Ville. Both are situated along the side of the port, taking in a very diverse population and numerous economic activities. They were therefore chosen, as well as the new quarters for the second period. Finally, it was a question of choosing the sources. In the absence of reliable continuing sources (such as ecclesiastical or hospital records), I chose legal documents, and in particular three sources little used to date in Marseilles: settled prices, inventories made after death, and leases. Very schematically, the first gives a description of the house and the second a description of the domestic decor. What interests us here is the leases. Their interest for an historian of housing accommodation is manifold. They describe the accommodation, and we know that in the modern period it has not necessarily been organized in the same way that it is today; they allow us to build up a history of rental values, of housing conditions for each social class and their geographical distribution. Numerous questions, to be dealt with usefully, must be based on a statistically viable amount of data. 2564 leases have therefore been collected, 1069 for the first period and 1495 for the second, stripping the records of about 200 registered notaries.

The manual manipulation of these 2560 records took a considerable amount of time. To extract all the information, it was necessary in effect to re-read the whole collection a number of times, to create a vast matrix for each interrogation, notching up the facts one at a time, and then to proceed to detailed calculations with all the risks of error attached to that method. I therefore turned to the computer for assistance.

3

Describing your world

There has been a long tradition of descriptive writing and of descriptive criticism that predates the use of computers. In this chapter we seek to locate our experimental classroom work using logic programming within this broader context.

George Orwell, in his essay 'Politics *vs* literature: an examination of *Gulliver's travels*', mounted an attack on both Swift's account of the Academy of Lagado and the philosophy that underlay Swift's writing. Professors in this academy

> "invent simplified languages, write books by machinery, educate their pupils by inscribing the lessons on a wafer and causing them to swallow it, or propose to abolish individuality altogether by cutting off part of the brain of one man and grafting it onto the head of another."

Orwell saw the implied aim as

> "a static, incurious civilisation — the world of his own day, a little cleaner, a little saner, with no radical change and no poking into the unknowable."

In his essay 'The prevention of literature" Orwell (Orwell, 1957) sees the arrival of mechanical writing:

> "Even more machine-like is the production of short stories, serials and poems for the very cheap magazines."

His analysis of 'Boys weeklies' (Orwell, 1957) could be applied to current video adventure games, with stereotyped characters, a small defined mental world, and a deliberate remoteness from real life, poorly written but influential:

> "the worst books are often the most important, because they are usually the ones that are read earliest in life."

In *'The road to Wigan pier'* Orwell (Orwell, 1962) expressed bitter views on machines that we can apply to computers in education:

"Like a drug, the machine is useful, dangerous and habit-forming".

"So long as the machine is there, one is under an obligation to use it".

The twin concerns for writing and for machines were taken up by Garth Boomer in his paper *Zen and the Art of Computing* (Boomer, 1983a). He crucially links the two.

"Writing is a machine in the sense that it is a rule-governed system for conveying meanings encoded in orthographic symbols."

Neither of them can be seen in isolation.

"Computers, like writing, should not be considered separately from the purposes and values being served."

Perhaps most importantly he sees 'machines' in a further sense.

"Before one can deal with computer education constructively, one must deal with the 'machine', the institution, within which computing will be taught. The art of educating must come of age before the art of computing has a chance."

The work described here has been carried out on the project 'Logic as a computer language of children', with the support of the Science and Engineering Research Council and the Nuffield Foundation. The concern has been for the descriptive use of logic in a way such that our descriptions are regarded by the computer as programs. The ideal would be for us to be able to use spoken or written natural language (and progress is being made to that end in Japan and elsewhere), but our work has involved the development of 'front-end' programs which can approximate to that objective and also provide a motivating environment for descriptive and creative writing. We have worked in the context of normal class teaching and the objectives of the schools concerned, in particular Park House Middle School, Wimbledon, Bishop Wand School, Sunbury, and Ricards Lodge High School, Wimbledon. I am greateful for the collaboration of Ken Della Rocca, Brian Pook, John Latham, Amanda Johnson, Inga Watson, and Bob Hurst.

There can be a problem in motivating imaginative descriptive writing. One method adopted by John Latham was to commence with a simple unexciting sentence, such as 'the house stood in the valley' and to seek to improve it. As further adjectives and adverbs were suggested a range of possible sentences using them syntactically correctly was generated on the computer. After using combinations of adjectives or adverbs, adjectival phrases and adverbial phrases were introduced. In the context of a story the writer might want to communicate a particular atmosphere. The students identified particular nice or nasty words that could be used to form nice or nasty descriptions. The objective was not a sophisticated computer program but a piece of descriptive writing into which more thought had been put than usual. A side-effect was the consideration of issues of grammar in the context of use.

This work has much in common with Chomsky's study of ordinary use of language, and his conclusion that "we are struck at once by its creative character, by the character of free creation within a system of rules". Chomsky's work was a major influence on the first implementor of the logic programming language PROLOG that we have been using.

A class of third-year pupils at Bishop Wand School, led by Amanda Johnson, was working on devising newspaper headlines and improvising short drama presentations on the theme of the accompanying article, prior to writing such articles themselves. Working in groups, they agreed on the allocation of character, relationships between characters, and to the sequence of events. One short drama concerned a terrorist car-bomber and two thieves who were blown up by the car bomb and then decorated for bravery by the Queen. One stage of the writing process was running the description of characters and events as a program, editing and amending it until it satisfied the group.

A class of final-year students at Park House Middle School has been concerned with collecting and using a mass of information about Third World countries, the arms race, and world hunger. Their lessons, led by Brian Pook, involve a good deal of discussion, written work, creative writing and artwork. They have developed computer programs using their information, making it easily accessible and usable for comparisons and answering particular questions. They can add the information in response to English questions where the form is known in advance, or by using a simple syntax if they are adding other information. Alternatively, having described the options open to the principal participants, as in the arms race, they can explore the consequences of different decisions. The computer can help raise the level of classroom discussion.

A class from Bishop Wand School had a week's field trip to Wales, taking with them five microcomputers on which to record their descriptions of what they saw. After the briefest of introductions to the computer they could enter their account of the slate mines, employment patterns, and the tourist industry. One group worked on developing a small 'expert system' to identify birds, using some of the expert knowledge of the Headmaster and the Mountain Centre Warden.

The use of this 'ideal type' kind of explanation has similarities with the use of historical drama, with the difference that a range of choices is open rather than predetermined. Furthermore, one student can write the adventure for another to play. Similarly the Welsh field trip can be written up as an adventure game (a guided tour, described by someone who has been, to be used as introduction to an intending participant). Such writing has a purpose and a perceived utility.

A new area that is currently developing is that of interactive problem-solving. We may seek advice regarding a particular problem that we face, and we can received help so long as we can in turn provide answers to particular questions. As an example I have represented Orwell's rules for translating English into Newspeak (from the Appendix to 1984) as a program which is used to build up a Newspeak dictionary. The user chooses an English word, and is asked for the core word on which it is based, the part of speech, whether it is positive or negative in tone, and the degree of emphasis. In return he is given the Newspeak translation, which is also added to the dictionary. We can translate from one language into another provided that we know the necessary dictionary meanings and follow the right grammatical rules. If we can describe a subject that we know about, it can be of use to others. Furthermore, if we start our description, it can then prompt us to give further detail of flesh out our account.

Work has begun on problems of text analysis and literary criticism. Many literary devices can be described in terms of patterns, and many dramatic plots are clarified by a description of the relationships between characters. We would like to have intelligent access to literary text on disk, and the capacity to add our own critical comments for purposes of analysis and teaching. The same opportunities will be open to students. This could potentially have a deep impact on the teaching of set texts, and of critical techniques. George Watson, in his history of descriptive criticism (Watson, 1962), says:

"It is about one thing, a given text to which critic and reader may appeal equally for confirmation."

Even the limited work done to date has raised serious issues. Work in the Indian Ocean island of Reunion using the computer for the representation and use of knowledge has emphasized

"the attention which must be paid to the cultural context of the experimental activity and of communication."

and is developing the means of communicating with the computer using the natural languages of French and Creole.

We must not accept unwanted cultural baggage as the cost of the computer. We must also be aware of further consequences: we are encouraging our students to describe and explain their world, to seek patterns and rules. We are encouraging the search for explanations to answers to questions, and the development of structures that can be used to help make sense of complex problems.

Garth Boomer identified many of the problems for schools of the active participatory approach to education that is being discussed here:

"The productive mode is always difficult in schools. Economically it means providing enough machines for students to use. Pedagogically it means having teachers who themselves know how to produce. Politically, it means handing over the means of production to the workers (a prelude to revolution?)."

An earlier version of this chapter was given as a paper at the 1984 Conference of the National Association for the Teaching of English.

4

Artificial intelligence and educational computing

Artificial Intelligence (AI) is a field where the state of the art is constantly changing, and it would be impossible to present a universally accepted overview at any given time. The account that follows is the view of a classroom history teacher whose attempts to use computers as a tool for teaching his subject have taken him into this new area, first as an outsider, and then as a participating researcher and research manager who has come to realise that others have come to the field from a vast variety of backgrounds but for analogous reasons, stemming from a dissatisfaction with conventional approaches to their particular intellectual concerns.

4.1 A NEW CENTRAL POSITION FOR ARTIFICIAL INTELLGENCE RESEARCH

Work in the field of AI is inherently controversial, involving as it does the apparently hubristic enterprise of constructing computer programs that model aspects of intelligent behaviour. The academic and general community has been divided for decades on the issue of what constitutes intelligence. As Fleck writes in his perceptive 'Development and establishment in artificial intelligence' (Fleck, 1982):

> "Intelligence is not a socially or cognitively well-defined goal, and every distinctive social group tends to have its own implicit definition, couched in terms of its own interests."

Given a lack of agreement on the nature of intelligence, there has been an understandable difficulty in obtaining cohesion and coordination for research in the area. At a time of financial stringency and of government scepticism regarding academic activities, there has been a problem as to how much autonomy should be exercised by the practitioners in this new field while they still conform to official requirements. There has also been a popular view, held by those proud of their Western humanist cultural tradition, that AI research is in some way threatening or even immoral. Indeed, for those used to scientific research based on the model of the physical sciences, AI can seem unfamiliar, diffuse, focusing on method rather than content.

Some common elements can be identified in the growing profusion of research in this new field. General purpose computers are used both as instruments for research and as deriving from a useful academic discipline. A range of new high-level list-processing languages has been developed as tools. Computers have been primarily used for non-numerical applications, with an emphasis on the logic and structure of the subject area under consideration. Particular skills or craft knowledge have developed in the community that have general application across the field. A range of new techniques has evolved, concerning problem solving, knowledge representation, knowledge acquisition and learning, and heuristics for intelligent searching. There has been an emphasis on the construction of computational models for intellectual processes, without a concern for the physiological aspect of such mechanisms. A wide range of separate research areas have evolved in the last twenty years, including natural language, game playing, theorem proving, cognitive modelling, and machine vision.

The activity of AI researchers has reflected a dissatisfaction with conventional numerically-oriented applications of computers. They have outlined ambitious research projects that have caught the popular imagination, as with, for instance, Donald Michie's pioneering proposals in robotics. All too often this has involved underestimating the time, difficulty, and cost of such research, and some sponsors have become disillusioned, reverting to the support of projects with more short-term limited objectives.

In 1972 the British Science Research Council commissioned a report by the eminent hydrodynamicist Sir James Lighthill on research in AI. His highly critical report (Lighthill, 1972) led to cuts in the funding of research in the United Kingdom, and the dissolution of a number of active research groups. Michie's Department of Machine Intelligence and Perception in Edinburgh became less prominent, and a number of leading British researchers such as Elcock left the country to establish new research groups overseas, particularly in North America. Work in cognitive sciences gained strength in the 1970s, particularly at the Universities of Sussex and Essex, but AI was left in an unstable condition, described by Fleck as:

> "an amazing state of substantive partisanship, or scientific ethnocentricity, in which proponents of the various different research areas each tend to see their own approach as the real AI approach."

AI research in the United States did not suffer the same fate, and enjoyed continued academic respectability and largely military funding. Many British researchers, disillusioned by the atomsphere following the Lighthill Report, found a welcome in flourishing American centres such as Stanford and MIT, or helped establish new research groups such as in Syracuse, Rochester, and Western

Ontario. By 1980 the first commercially viable 'expert systems' were beginning to emerge, dealing with medical diagnosis (for example, MYCIN) and mineral prospecting (for example, PROSPECTOR).

4.2 THE JAPANESE FIFTH GENERATION COMPUTING PROJECT

How is it, then, that though the majority of AI research activity was focused in the United States during the 1970s, AI now occupies a central place in most national plans for economic development involving computer science research? A major role, has been played by the Japanese proposals for 'fifth generation' computer systems. The publication of the proposals was preceded by an exhaustive survey of international academic research, with special attention being paid to developments in American expert systems.

The Japanese were motivated by a desire to set the lead in this new field rather than continuing to be subordinate to American academic and commercial direction. What was proposed was an explicit scientific revolution in contrast to previous minor design changes in computer technology. The proposals were spelt out in a May 1982 publication of the Japanese Institute for New Generation Computer Technology (ICOT):

> "The changes from one generation to the next in computer technology have so far been made to accommodate changes in device technology, that is from vacuum tubes to transistors, then integrated circuits, and recently to large-scale integrated circuits. Such hindsight tells us, then, that there have been no major changes in the basic design philosophy and utilization objectives of computers.
>
> With fifth generation computers, however, the expected generational change is more like a 'generic change' which involves not only a change in device technology, to very large scale integrated circuits (VLSI), but also simultaneous changes in design philospophy and in fields of application." (ICOT, 1982)

A new approach to the use of computers is proposed for a number of application fields in the 1990s, involving a change from machines centred around numerical computations to machines that can:

> "assess the meaning of information and understand the problems to be solved."

To accomplish this change a number of developments are required; in the words of the ICOT report:

> "1. To realize basic mechanisms for inference, association, and learning in hardware and make them the core functions of the fifth generation computers.
> 2. To prepare basic artificial intelligence software to fully utilize the above functions.

3. To take advantage of pattern recognition and artificial intelligence research achievements, and realize man–machine interfaces that are natural to man.
4. To realize support systems for resolving the 'software crisis' and enhancing software production."

The Japanese identified a particular British and European research activity as central to their proposals. Logic programmers, regarded as heretics even in the AI community, were suddenly thrust into a prominent position as technical innovation made their goals closer to being achievable. Fuchi's important paper 'Aiming for knowledge information processing systems' (Fuchi, 1981) makes explicit the importance given to logic programming and its research tradition.

"PROLOG (PROgramming in LOGic) seems to be the best suited as the starting point in considering new base languages for knowledge information processing. . . ."
". . . while the route to knowledge information processing is an advance to a new age, it can also be viewed as representing the inheritance and development of the legacies of the past from the viewpoint of research efforts."

4.3 THE ALVEY REPORT AND ITS IMPLEMENTATION

The British Government commissioned the report of the Alvey Committee in 1982 to consider a response to the Japanese initiative and offers of collaboration in research. They recommended a new emphasis on the study of "intelligent knowledge-based systems" (IKBS), agreeing with the Japanese that:

"We want more powerful information processing systems with a more effective transfer of human intelligence and knowledge to the computer."
(Alvey, 1982)

A major collaborative research programme on a national basis was proposed, with explicitly radical implications for education in terms of allocation of resources and curriculum content. Disparate areas of activity were suddenly accorded a new respectability and cohesion, and conventional practices were thrown into question.

In their paragraph concerning schools, the Alvey Committee were extremely critical of current approaches to educational computing, in particular involving the teaching of BASIC:

"Action must start in the schools. We support the moves which are now putting computing on the curriculum. But, it is no good just providing schools with microcomputers. This will merely produce a generation of poor BASIC programmers. Universities in fact are having to give remedial education to entrants with 'A' level Computer Science. Teachers must be properly trained, and the languages chosen with an eye to the future. Uncorrected, the explosion in home computing with its 1950s and 1960s programming style will make this problem even worse. Action is also needed to increase the stock of computer science teachers by training existing teachers of other subjects in computer science and by encouraging young computer science graduates to enter teaching. The teaching of computer science in schools must be increased substantially, in quality and in quantity".

Unusually, a long-term view was taken. AI and other research activities were not expected to give instant solutions to ancient problems, but distinct targets were identified and timetables suggested for five- and ten-year projects.

The Alvey Report was substantially accepted by government which agreed that some 350 million pounds should be devoted to the effort over five years. They insisted on a greater degree of financial commitment by participating companies, and a correspondingly reduced role for government expenditure. In the early stages of the resulting Alvey Programme for Advanced Information Technology the research direction has been less focussed than in Japan, and companies have been more concerned with short-time financial survival and early marketable products. Government expenditure cuts have in fact reduced the numbers of graduates in computer science being produced, and no major research has been supported in education, partly through a lack of commercial preparedness to support research without a real prospect of considerable financial profit from sales of educational software. Schools have been provided with hundreds of thousands of reduced-price British microcomputers in a scheme devised to aid the promising British microcomputer hardware industry. The Microelectronics Education Programme (MEP) has striven to provide short courses for teachers and some educational software, but without a basis of sound research and with woefully inadequate funds.

4.4 THE INTERNATIONAL POSITION

Internationally the position is similar. AI has moved to centre stage in advanced research supported both by governments and private industry. In Europe the ESPRIT programme has a similar brief to the Alvey Programme, and individual European countries have their own research programmes, as do Australia, Israel, and Canada. Major American companies such as IBM, Honeywell, DEC, Texas Instruments, and Burroughs are working both individually and in collaboration, with considerable research funding from the American Department of Defense. Again, though students now in schools and colleges will be the users of the new fifth generation computers, there has been little emphasis to date on education, though many millions of microcomputers are now in educational use internationally.

4.5 INFLUENCES OF AI ON EDUCATIONAL COMPUTING

It may be helpful to draw some distinctions between the starting-point of work in conventional educational computing and work in AI in education. I am aware that some work is not so easily classified, and indeed a great deal is to be learned from the writings of those such as Hartley (Hartley, 1981a, b) and Self (Self,

1979, Self, forthcoming) who have sought to broaden the context within which they were working. My account owes a great deal to earlier accounts of the field by Howe (Howe, 1978a), Ross (Ross, 1980), Rushby (Rushby, 1979), and Kemmis (Kemmis, 1977), and to visits to the research groups at Edinburgh, Sussex, Chelsea, Exeter, Hull, Cardiff, Southampton, Massachusetts Institute of Technology, Stanford, Syracuse, Rochester, Western Ontario, Rutgers, New Mexico, Virginia Polytechnic, Marseilles, Aix, La Trobe, Monash, Melbourne Institute of Technology, Sydney, Auckland, Christchurch, and Tokyo. I cannot hope to do justice to all of the work being carried out, but my experience confirms Fleck's view of AI as

> "a shared body of technique and practice . . . transmitted by apprenticeship and personnel migration"

where

> "access to this body of knowledge and skill is restricted by the need for first-hand contact and for adequate computing factilites, consequently leading to tight intercentre and intergenerational linkages in the area."

The shared perspective on AI in education has become more evident in the United Kingdom in recent conference and publications (Yazdani, 1984, Ramsden, 1984, Torrance, 1984, O'Shea & Self, 1983, Sage & Smith, 1983).

4.6   THE STARTING POINT OF CONVENTIONAL EDUCATIONAL COMPUTING

In simple terms we might agree that conventional educational computing has been concerned with exploiting at any given time the facilities offered by a particular generation of computers, making use of the technology in the classroom. This has been analogous to the use of language laboratories and teaching machines, or at a less ambitious and less specifically designed level, of tape recorders, film and slide projectors, or even overhead projectors and various kinds of writing surface down to blackboards and chalk. Practitioners have often required general expertise in educational technology: less technically adventurous teachers have remained content with chalk and talk and have retained suspicions even of white washable boards on which felt pens can be used. There have indeed been limitations of the technology, and educational side-effects of its incorporation into the teacher's armoury, in terms of the constraints it may impose upon teaching method, lesson content, and classroom activity.

4.7   THE STARTING POINT FOR AI IN EDUCATION

The starting point in AI is different, with its focus on the analysis of human learning activity. As Margaret Boden writes in *Artificial Intelligence and Natural Man* (Boden, 1977):

"Artificial Intelligence is not the study of computers, but of intelligence in thought and action. Computers are its tools, because its theories are expressed as computer programs that enable machines to do things that would require intelligence if done by people."

Workers in the field are concerned to model and extend the effectiveness of learning, with the computer available as a powerful tool in both of these enterprises.

4.8 THE IMPORTANCE OF EDUCATIONAL PSYCHOLOGY AND COGNITIVE SCIENCE

The application of AI research in education owes a considerable debt to educational psychology and cognitive science, which should be given primacy in the educational context over computer science considerations. In return it provides a medium in which theories can recognizably be formulated and formalized, constructively compared and subjected to practical tests of efficacy.

The influence of Piaget (Piaget, 1926, 1928, 1950, 1970, 1971, Piaget & Inhelder, 1958) has been enormous, with his formalization of developmental stages in adolescent intellectual development.

Bruner (Bruner, 1960, 1968, 1972) has provoked considerable activity in the field of knowledge representation and its more radical classroom implications (Rogers, 1978) together with far-reaching proposals for restructuring the school curriculum and its modes of teaching (Wolsk, 1975).

Gagne (Gagne, 1967, 1975) has brought to bear the concepts of information processing on the educational or instructional context, though this has yet to be developed satisfactorily in the English classroom. Pask (Pask, 1970, Pask & Curran, 1982) has written extensively on conceptual networks, conversational theory and, with Scott (Pask & Scott, 1972), on cognitive styles, but his work has often been perceived as too abstract for practical application. The computer has the potential to give concrete form to his abstractions, previously represented almost mystically as exhibitions of sculptured mobiles in the milieux of art galleries.

Kelly (Kelly, 1955), Bannister & Fransella (Bannister & Fransella, 1971), Ryle (Ryle, 1975), and Shaw (Shaw, 1979) have explored extensively the potential of personal construct theory, but have lacked the means of demonstrating their theories in action to sceptical classroom practitioners.

4.9 THE DEVELOPMENT OF CONVENTIONAL EDUCATIONAL COMPUTING

Conventional educational computing, with its use of drill-and-practice programs, and a sequential approach to the exploration of selected content within a subject domain, grew naturally from the behaviourist psychology of Skinner, and its automation in the form of programmed learning. The student is faced with a pre-prepared 'frame' of stimulus materials, to which he is expected to make one of a selected range of responses. Correct responses are rewarded by praise, and pre-set routing algorithms direct the student to his next task, either in strict linear progression or with some element of 'branching' arising from the computer analysis of the level of competence achieved to date.

In many cases programmed learning texts could achieve the same result — the use of a computer system can minimize the chances of error when the intervention of the teacher may be considered an unnecessary distraction. The advent of cheap microcomputers has meant that in many cases such drill-and-practice programs, or linear 'simulation' packages, have been transferred from minicomputers, often in an abbreviated form for reasons of limitations of space in the microcomputer, and only belatedly if at all taking advantage of further facilities of the microcomputers such as graphics and colour.

4.10   CRITICISMS OF CONVENTIONAL EDUCATIONAL COMPUTING

There have been dissenting voices in recent years. Howe and Du Boulay (Howe & Du Boulay, 1979) expressed scepticism about the immediate benefits of technological innovation:

> "Technological innovations have much less impact than their proponents had hoped."

and fear that the widespread use of drill-and-practice programs would

> "amount to turning the clock back to an earlier era in education."

Events in the subsequent five years suggest that their pessimism was not entirely misplaced, for the use of drill-and-practice has conflicted with the concern of classroom teachers to emphasize understanding, rather than rote learning of some arbitrarily assembled collection of 'facts'.

Hartley (Hartley, 1981a, b) has emphasized the importance of the role of the learner, crucial to Piagetian child-centred discovery approaches to education:

> "Only by allowing the student himself to make choices, to justify them and see their effects, will he learn about the process of making educational decisions; only in this way will he become self-evaluative and learn how to learn."

In a critique of programs developed on the National Development Program for Computer Assisted Learning, Hartley (Hartley 1981a) focused on another point which was developed also by Self (Self, 1979). The behaviourist approach of rewarding the correct response fails to give support to students in difficulty who give other responses. Teachers are increasingly concerned with diagnosing children's difficulties and taking appropriate remedial action. For this the teacher requires an adequate model of the student. Taking up Hartley's plea for the student to be given the initiative in interactions with the computer, he suggests that:

"We could . . . hope to maintain a more sophisticated interaction by monitoring the student's proposed course of action, for example, by using the student model and the learning model to predict the likely outcome of the course of action."

The objectives are described by Self in educational rather than technical terms:

"One of the benefits which may well derive from this work is in making human teachers more understanding about a student's difficulties and problems."

4.11   SIMULATION IN ARTIFICIAL INTELLIGENCE

A major theme of both recent classroom activity and AI research has been the simulation of behaviour to aid its understanding. It may be instructive to describe an example from the AI literature that is unlikely to be familiar to practitioners of educational computing.

Abelson (Abelson, 1973) wrote a fascinating paper on 'The structure of belief systems' where he approached a familiar topic, the ideological conflict of the cold war, from an unusual perspective, that of the cognitive scientist. Using his experience and that of his colleagues he analysed the cognitive limitations faced by human agents in the face of transient, unfamilar, noisy, and competitive information. In order to examine such limitations in action he constructed what he called the 'ideology machine':

"The Ideology Machine is a model of certain aspects of a True Believer, and is presently set up to simulate resonses to foreign policy questions by a right-wing ideologue, such as Barry Goldwater. The simplified simulation of a Cold War Warrior has stored in it the vocabulary, conceptual categories, episodes and master script appropriate to arch-conservative views. If the contents of memory were suitably changed, any other ideological system of comparable simplicity could be simulated with the same computer program."

In order to pass a 'Turing test' (Turing, 1950) of authenticity, the ideology machine was to be subjected to the same form of questionning as a State Department spokesman. The forms were as follows, with 'E' representing 'Event', and 'A' representing 'Foreign Policy Actors':

"1. Is E credible? That is, could E happen or have happended?
2. If and when E, what will happen?
3. If and when E, what should A do?
4. When E, what should A have done?
5. How come E? That is, what caused E, or what is E meant to accomplish?
6. Sir, would you please comment on E."

Controversially, Abelson identifies a master script that applies, he says, to many ideological systems:

"The bad guys have evil plans which are succeeding, and only the good guys can stop them. Unfortunately, the good guys haven't done it yet, and the reason is that the bad guys have the help of dupes, fools, lackeys and the running dogs who wittingly or unwittingly interfere with the efforts of the good guys. The only hope, therefore, is to raise the wrath of the people against the bad guys and their puppets."

There is considerable scope for educational applications of such an approach to simulation. The present writer has developed (Ennals, 1979a, 1979b, 1980, 1981a, 1982a, 1982d) experience-centred classroom activities where participants take on the roles of historical agents within a particular situation such as the Norman Conquest, the Wedgwood Pottery firm in the eighteenth century, the Russian Revolution, or the European Parliament.

4.12   HISTORICAL SIMULATION AND ARTIFICIAL INTELLIGENCE

A curious academic phenomenon in recent years has been that researchers in AI and historical simulation have been separately drawing on the same ideas and sources. This is Jon Doyle of Massachusetts Institute of Technology AI Laboratory, referring to Collingwood in his *A model for deliberation, action and introspection* (Doyle, 1980):

"Collingwood (Collingwood, 1946) suggested that the aim of history is not just to record annals, but to discover psychological explanations of the actions of men. This involves not only discovering the facts of a situation, but also the ways the participants viewed the situation and the possible actions available to them. That is, the goal of the historian is to infer the attitudes or mental states of each of the participants in the event."

In the same year Jon Nichol, a prolific author of classroom history textbooks, wrote a pamphlet for the Historical Association entitled "Simulation in History Teaching: a practical approach" in which, from a similar theoretical and philosophical background, he writes (Nichol, 1980):

"Simulation has a major role in 'breathing life into' classroom history. In a simulation the pupil takes the role of an historical character, and has to take a decision or a series of decisions similar to those which faced people in the past. Simulations produce the teaching opportunities for the affective development of students. A simulation provides the structure for imaginative, sympathetic and empathetic work. It helps to produce a solution to the problem of carrying into practice the desirable but apparently unattainable goal of children realistically deploying historical imagination."

The concepts of simulation can be applied not only to the reconstruction of historical events, but also to an analysis of the work of expert historians. Teachers of history in the tradition of the 'new history' (Booth, 1969, 1978, Dickinson & Lee, 1977, 1984, Shemilt, 1980) have focused attention on research methods, the use of evidence, and the drawing of appropriate conclusions from incomplete information. This work has been done without computers, but provides an excellent context for current activities. The clearest evidence for this view lies in the current work in Exeter directed by Jon Nichol, and in New South Wales coordinated by Bryan Cowling, Yvonne Larsson, and Paul Fennell, again using PROLOG.

Jon Nichol has found in his Exeter History and Humanities Project that PROLOG and the microcomputer can provide valuable classroom assistance. He can use available tools to explore both his own subject and other across the curriculum in the way he wants, without compromising his own educational criteria for the treatment of the subject or pedagogical approach (Nichol & Dean 1984a, b, c).

4.13   RADICAL ALTERNATIVES TO CONVENTIONAL EDUCATIONAL COMPUTING: THE WORK OF SEYMOUR PAPERT

In conventional classroom terms the most widespread radical alternative approach to date has arisen from the work of Seymour Papert at Massachusetts Institute of Technology and then for a brief period at the French Centre Mondial de Programmation.

One indication of the progress of such work based on ideas of AI is the change in tone of a rival innovator, Patrick Suppes of Stanford. He wrote in 1972 (Suppes & Morningstar, 1972):

"The greatest block to individualized instruction is not the limitations of computer technology as such, but rather the absence of tough-minded intellectual studies of how we can do it."

In 1979, in a review of current trends in Computer-Assisted Instruction (Suppes, 1979) he wrote:

"We should expect by 1990 CAI courses of considerable pedagogical and psychological sophistication. The student should expect penetrating and sophisticated things to be said to him about the character of his work, and to be disappointed when the CAI courses with which he is interacting do not have such features."

By 1982 he was taking steps to incorporate the results of such work into courses produced by his firm, Computer Curriculum Corporation, to supplement the wide range of sophisticated computer-assisted packages developed for secondary school and college use. As Professor of Mathematics and Logic in the Institute for Mathematics in the Social Sciences, he has for many years used computer programs to teach his courses in logic and set theory, leaving him free to do other things while carrying an unusually heavy teaching load in official eyes.

Seymour Papert's ideas are most accessibly developed in his book *Mindstorms* (Papert, 1980), where computers are presented as "carriers of powerful ideas and of the seeds of cultural change". He sees an innovative approach to the curriculum as following from experience with computers:

"They can help people form new relationships with knowledge that cuts across the traditional lines separating humanities from sciences and knowledge of the self from both of these."

After many years of collaborative research with Piaget in Geneva he is also concerned to use computers to "challenge current beliefs about who can understand what and at what age". In a sense he regards the traditional teacher as his test case, as he wonders

"whether we can construct intellectual environments in which people who today think of themselves as 'humanist' will feel part of, not alienated from, the process of constructing computational cultures".

The book is full of controversial, almost visionary statements. Teachers brought up on a diet of Piagetian ages and stages may appreciate Papert's thoughts on concrete and formal operations:

"The computer can concretize (and personalize) the formal, . . . it can allow us to shift the boundary separating concrete and formal. Knowledge that was accessible only through formal processes can now be approached concretely. And the real magic comes from the fact that this knowledge includes those elements one needs to become a formal thinker."

Papert sees his ideas as helpful in the teaching of the traditional curriculum, but says

"I have thought of it as a vehicle for Piagetian learning, which to me is learning without curriculum."

The principal area of the curriculum to which it has been applied is Euclidean geometry, which is taught by the student learning to program a 'turtle' which draws geometrical figures, although in theory the potential applications of LOGO, particularly with the handicapped (Weir, 1981), are much broader. Extensions of LOGO now under development, and experimental use, offer considerably greater potential in areas such as art and music, in physics, and to a certain extent in creative writing.

4.14   EVALUATIONS OF LOGO

LOGO has been the focus of considerable enthusiasm in recent years, often with inadequate testing and evaluation. A notable exception to this is the work at Edinburgh University directed by Jim Howe, where considerable experience has been built up in the use of LOGO with children of a variety of ages, with the handicapped, and in teacher training, though the widespread use of this research has been restricted by the delays in implementations for microcomputers, by the differences in the versions of LOGO produced for different machines, and by the limited extent of involvement of ordinary classroom teachers in the design and direction of the projects. This last defect has diminished somewhat with the recent MEP experimental work in Hatfield coordinated by Richard Noss, a classroom mathematics teacher. The Edinburgh approach has often been less radical than Papert's ambitious ideas cited above, and they have evaluated their work in terms of its effectiveness at teaching certain restricted areas of the conventional curriculum (Howe, O'Shea, & Plane, 1979). Some scepticism can also be detected in schools when they note the small group sizes that have been assumed, and the extensive continuing involvement of university researchers in the trial schools. Now, however, teachers and lecturers are taking this powerful tool and employing it to excellent effect in practical work with children (Ross, 1983, Adams & McDougall, 1983, Goodyear, 1984).

In France the Centre Mondial de Programmation undertook an extensive programme of experimental use and evaluation of LOGO with the services of Seymour Papert as Director in association with Jean-Jacques Servan-Schreiber, who had an elaborate vision of the liberating potential of computers (Servan-Schreiber, 1981). Most of the experimental activities have now ceased. They included 'flooding' the Marseilles suburb of Belle-de-Mai (equivalent to Liverpool's Toxteth, New York's Harlem, or London's Brixton) with 'turtles' and experimentally observing the outcome, with a vast team of untrained researchers, devoid of contacts with the local educational or computer science communities. In Senegal LOGO was introduced in the Wolof language, and in La Reunion in Creole — the local version is known as POC-POC (Vogel, 1983). An evaluation conference was held in Clermont-Ferrand in December 1982, and the reports were not encouraging. Harald Wertz reported (Wertz, 1982), and I have here translated some of his remarks:

> "Every time, if one looks at the computer products of the pupils, the complexity of their programs, one is struck by the uniformity of the results and by the wretchedness of the programs. Naturally one possible hypothesis would be that the processes of problem solving are themselves very simple and limited. This strikes me, in the light of current knowledge, as being to simple. Another hypothesis would be that the computer facilities placed at the disposal of these people are too limited and impose too much 'computer' thinking (as opposed to simply thinking) on the programmers, and that the uniformity of the results (in LOGO it is rare to see programs which escape from the 'square' and the 'house') is only a direct reflection of the weakness of the means at their disposal and the inadequacy of such computational constructs (and these languges) for expressing the mechanisms of problem-solving."

There had been a tragic mismatch between potential and expectation. In many cases, such as Belle-de-Mai, the specification documents describing the problems to be dealt with were clear and explicit (much of the text could be run directly as PROLOG databases!), but the LOGO turtle was hideously inadequate to deal with the diversity of problems, particularly in the hands of unprepared researchers. In this case a report by Professor Michael Griffiths led to the project being closed. Nationally, Seymour Papert parted company with Centre Mondial, and without his presence and that of his colleagues many other projects have foundered.

4.15   ARTIFICIAL INTELLIGENCE IN THE CLASSROOM

There has been something of a general crisis of expectations in the field of computers in education. The cost of computer hardware has suddenly fallen so that access to the technology is a feasible option for schools and even for individuals, yet the availability of software has been such that teachers have questioned the educational validity of the use of computers, or have expressed frustration at their inability to carry out their ambitious plans for teaching their subjects in a new way.

One problem has been that the development work in sophisticated computer-based learning in the past has been based on larger machines, often with time-sharing use of a minicomputer. The cost of such equipment kept it out of the reach of the average school, and the activity had the status of research. Where larger systems have been used with children, as with the products of research at Stanford (Suppes, 1979), and with PLATO (Alpert & Bitzer, 1970), the educational objectives have been modest. More ambitious work with a foundation in AI has required considerable involvement of research staff, and has not typically been envisaged for use with full classes of children with the normal class teacher in control. Teachers with access to the literature may have read about SCHOLAR (Carbonnel, 1970), SOPHIE (Brown *et al.* 1975), MYCROFT (Goldstein, 1975), and programs developed on the National Development Program for Computer Assisted Learning, but they have not yet been available for general use.

In consequence there has been a tendency for schools, computer manufacturers, software houses, and publishers to remain conservation in outlook, acting on the assumption that conventional programs and the availability of the language BASIC for use by the non-specialist was as much as could be expected. It has difficult for teachers to gain access to practical use of an alternative AI approach, and even discussion has been limited in popular magazines and journals.

There is no longer any reason for such a blinkered approach. Two AI languages are widely implemented on a large range of microcomputers used in schools, LOGO and PROLOG, and there is a rapidly expanding basis of practical classroom experience on which to build.

Other languages and tools derived from AI research should soon be available. Considerable work has been done, particularly at Sussex, with the language POP-2 (Sloman, 1978), originally developed in Edinburgh, which may soon be available for microcomputers as GLUE (Thorne, 1982). The leading American AI language LISP (McCarthy *et al.* 1962) is becoming available on microcomputers, but there is as yet little published information about its use with children. LOGO is originally a derivative of LISP, but has now a life of its own. Xerox have invested many years of research in the development of SMALLTALK (Goldberg, 1979) which has justly attracted considerable interest in Japan and elsewhere for its power and ease of use. It is not yet generally available, though its influence has been enormous on new systems such as the LISA and MACINTOSH produced by Apple, and in educational use in North America and Australia.

There are further obstacles in the way of such innovations, some of which have been analysed by Rushby (Rushby, 1981). There are of course the normal institutional and personal obstacles, as well as the problem of evaluating an activity which conforms to a different set of paradigms from that which has preceded it (Kuhn, 1970, Lakatos, 1976). Kemmis (Kemmis, 1977) and Rushby (Rushby, 1979) are helpful on this point, and there is a growing literature concerning approaches to evaluation, together with an increasingly informed educational community within which such criteria as are appropriate can be applied.

As is explicit in Papert's *Mindstorms* and in much of the foregoing analysis, the use of teaching methods and materials derived from AI brings with it an inescapable analysis of the nature of learning and its mode of development in the education systems of the world. We are not here merely discussing a passing technical phase, but the education of present and future children. The new powerful tools are now available, if we have the intellectual courage to put them to use.

4.16 AREAS OF CONTROVERSY IN ARTIFICIAL INTELLIGENCE RESEARCH

In this section I would like to discuss some controversial areas of AI, illustrating the points with examples from work in classrooms using LOGO and PROLOG. We must retain the context, established earlier, of AI as a craft activity, carried out in a community with common interests, within the framework of a collection of different research programs that may at times appear to compete, if only for the allocation of scarce resources.

4.17 KNOWLEDGE REPRESENTATION

A fundamental issue that has long divided the community is that of knowledge representation. In broad terms the main tradition has been to represent knowledge procedurally, as is seen in LOGO, where the emphasis is on building procedures for performing operations, which may themselves be defined in terms of other procedures. This was used as the basis of an AI text edited at Edinburgh by Bundy (Bundy, 1978) for use with undergraduates. This is consistent with conventional programming, where a program consists of a set of instructions to the computer as to how to perform a particular operation, which may be structured in terms of procedures.

There has been an alternative declarative tradition of knowledge representation, based on clear descriptions of information, often in terms of relationships between entities. Here we are concerned with the nature of a problem area, rather than with the mode of solution of a problem. Kowalski (Kowalski, 1974, 1979) proposed that descriptions could be regarded as programs if they were expressed in a form of logic that was understood by the computer. It can be perfectly natural to describe information using logic, and most academic disciplines place a value on such an activity. Children or teachers in the classroom can give a clear description of some subject with which they are concerned, and the computer takes that as a program to enable it to answer questions or solve problems concerning that subject.

The user, particularly the naive user, does not have to be concerned with the manner in which the computer executes a program. At a time when computer architecture is undergoing fundamental changes, the user can focus his attention on the form of his chosen subject, and disregard the machine except as a means of automatically providing the required information or output. This does not prejudice the simultaneous or subsequent learning of a computer language, but places the emphasis on clear thinking within a subject, rather than intruding extra levels of conceptual difficulty in the classroom. In computer science terms the student is developing a specification, with the added advantage that it can be run as a program to test its correctness.

4.17 CHALLENGES FOR EDUCATIONAL PSYCHOLOGY

Piagetian educational and cognitive psychology has been under attack (Peel, 1960, 1967, Donaldson, 1978), as any orthodoxy should be. Work using logic as a computer language with children, together within Papert's emphasis on the developmental implications of computing, provides a fascinating opportunity. Children can learn a form of expression, of knowledge representation, in one part of their school curriculum, which they can intuitively apply to other areas. We can model the sequence of logical operations described by Piaget, provide a more concrete representation of the different developmental stages, and have a new tool for investigating the mysterious observed phenomenon of 'decallage', whereby the orthodoxy is that the same child achieves formal operational thinking in mathematics at the age of 12, but in history not until the age of 15. Educational psychologists are beginning to respond to the challenge. Geoff Cumming at La Trobe University Melbourne, David Smith and colleagues at Southampton University, David Sewell and colleagues at Hull University, John Black and Art Graesser at Yale, Jon Nichol and colleagues at Exeter University Josie Taylor and colleagues at Sussex University, and groups led by Marc Eisenstadt and Tim O'Shea at the Open University, are concerning themselves with cognitive aspects of the educational use of logic programming.

4.19 CHALLENGES FOR THE SCHOOL CURRICULUM

The school curriculum faces a challenge, both from Papert's approach to the development of Piagetian ideas, and from the radical proposals by Bruner for a 'spiral curriculum' (Bruner, 1972), with the consequent erosion of traditional barriers between the disciplines. Classroom work with LOGO and PROLOG has inevitably thrown these barriers into question, while also providing tools for representing the knowledge of expert practitioners of particular disciplines in what have been fashionably known as 'expert systems' (Hammond, 1980,

1982a, b, Clark, McCabe & Hammond, 1981, Steel, 1981). The computer is not the subject of study, but provides tools with which traditional subjects can be better explored.

There is a final controversy regarding emphasis on the roles of the different participants in the education process. Are we to follow Piaget and centre our focus on the child, or, with Hirst, to emphasize forms of knowledge (Hirst, 1973)? Should we be providing a tool for the teacher, or a means of freeing the individual for a personal educational experience? What significance should be accorded to the computer, especially once the novelty of its use has worn off?

This activity of intelligent educational computing is in its infancy, and we have only begun to explore the alternatives and implications.

An earlier version of this chapter, entitled 'Artificial Intelligence', was published in the Pergamon Infotech State of the Art Report on Computer-Based Learning, edited by N. J. Rushby, in 1983.

5

Logic and logic programming

This chapter has two purposes. The first is to locate the activity of logic programming in a context in the history of ideas, and in particular the tradition concerned with the formalizing of human reasoning using logic. The second is to harness the skills and enthusiasms of trained minds to the development of a new field: the intelligent use of computers to assist in the solution of everyday human problems. Logic programming has been identified as the core of the new fifth generation of computers that are now under development. Hardware development is proceeding as planned, and costs are falling. New powerful programming tools are on the way, drawing their power from logic. At this stage a training in logical thinking begins to count more than a conventional grounding in computer science.

5.1 CONTEXT IN THE HISTORY OF IDEAS

Logic is a very old science. Over two thousand years ago Aristotle focused on the idea of 'following from' — the notion of logical consequence, that is the central idea of logic. The attention of the logician has been only on the form of the assertion that he is dealing with, not the content but only the form. Through Socratic syllogisms, Aristotelian laws of thought, and medieval scholasticism, were developed means of classifying and checking arguments.

Leibniz took the idea further, and dreamt of mechanizing deductive reasoning. He wrote "How much better will it be to bring under mathematical laws human reasoning which is the most excellent and useful thing we have". This would enable the mind to "be freed from having to think directly of things themselves, and yet everything will turn out correctly". His actual achievements were disappointing, though he had taken the enormous step of conceiving of logic as a deductive science.

Frege explicitly built on Leibniz's work, stating his intention to "express a content through written signs in a more precise and clear way than it is possible to do through words". He developed an artificial language that can be seen as the ancestor of systems of mathematical logic and of computer programming languages. The practical impact of these ideas at the time was limited, as they were very advanced, and seen as obscure and impenetrable. The brilliant mathematician Godel, writing in 1944 about Leibniz and Frege, provides the context in terms of a history of ideas were ahead of their time:

"Leibniz did not in his writings . . . speak of a utopian project; if we are to believe his words he had developed his calculus of reasoning to a large extent, but was waiting with its publication till the seed could fall on fertile ground."

Godel has recieved considerable attention for his work on Incompleteness. It is his work on Completeness that has provided much of the basis for the work of Alan Robinson. Many logicians had been waiting impatiently for the computer to become a practical tool. Several, such as Gilmore and Wang, made immediate use of early computers, writing down almost verbatim the methods Godel, Herbrand, and Skolem had described in the pre-computer age. The algorithms that Godel and Herbrand described were for the human computer, not an automatic machine but a person systematically following a plan of work. It had always seemed to be a possibility that you might be able to make a machine do that too. Paul Gilmore's first attempts were successful, but extremely slow. Martin Davis and Hilary Putnam were able to change Gilmore's programming in a minor way and to produce an enormous improvement. Robinson was able to take further unknown work by Herbrand and make dramatic further improvements in the performance of the same algorithm. Robinson's exposition in 1965 of the resolution principle led first to an explosion of interest in mechanical theorem-proving, and then to the development of logic programming, with the first implementation of PROLOG (PROgramming in LOGic) in Marseille in 1972.

Robinson assessed the current position in his paper *Logical Reasoning in Machines*:

"We seem now to be in a plateau where we are not gaining very much more of that sort of advantage but we are finding that the algorithm in the form that we now have it is surprixingly useful. We are beginnning to discover all sorts of unexpected uses for it, one of which is as the inner engine of a new way of programming, a new kind of computation facility which appears to have many remarkable advantages."

Robinson sees logicians as concerned with form, using variables to express generality by showing patterns which fit infinitely many cases. They catalogue logical forms, which are capable of being represented symbolically as data structures — matrices, lists, and other kinds of data structures that you can completely represent inside computers or on paper. Given the right ideas about representation, then operations or manipulations can be performed on the represented forms, just like any other data. Thus, because of the manner in which that form can be handled concretely, there is really no mystery about what logical reasoning, as seen by the computational logicians, really is. It is just a kind of data processing.

Computers do not have to imitate the way that humans do things, although of course the great precedent for all this is that humans have been doing it for a long time. One of the problems with Gilmore's early program was that it was put into the computer in the form in which it was originally devised, a human-oriented form. A general point applies to all kinds of computing: Do it the best way you can, whether or not it is simulating the way humans do it.

An important point made by Robinson, crucial to the present author's work in educational computing, is that in order to find the machine's answer useful to you, you do not have to know how it arrived at the answers. You can certainly use the answer that a proof-finding machine gives you, if it does give you one, because it is a proof. That is what proofs are for. They are devices for acting on the human data processing system.

A further crucial distinction must be made between the context of discovery and the context of justification. The context of discovery, searching for a proof, may be mysterious, involving guesswork and creativity. One beauty of the theorem-proving problem is that the messiness of discovery can be ignored. Our interest is in the outcome, which can be understood however it was discovered. We can all understand the proof, provided it is short and simple, of theorems that have frustrated logicians for centuries.

A similar analysis can be applied to the construction of 'expert systems', or 'intelligent knowledge based systems'. Typically such a system will consist of a collection of assertions gathered together in a knowledge base — the facts, definitions, and heuristics relating to that particular subject. We also have an inference engine, where the reasoning takes place. What happens is that the inference engine takes into account simply the form of the particular problem, the theorem to be proved or the question to be answered, and whatever is relevant from the knowledge base, again by virtue of its form and not its content. The machine does not know or care what you are talking about. It covers only whether what you say follows from what you have agreed to assume. Our machine restricts the problems of search by only following one kind of inference rule-resolution. It is a rule of inference that Robinson has codified and described exactly, which is adequate all by itself as the only rule needed in predicate calculus; embodied in the unification algorithm.

Robert Kowalski, now of Imperial College, gave a computational interpretation to these logical systems, which he called 'logic programming'. At the same time Alain Colmerauer and his colleagues in Marseille implemented this idea as PROLOG. The programmer user of PROLOG thinks that what he is doing is programming a machine that will then run on data, but the programming actually consists of asserting things into the knowledge base. The program simply consists of assertions that you believe are true about your problem domain. You then form your questions in such a way that it is an input to the program, and the act of getting the answers is the running of the program for that input.

The principal PROLOG implementer, David Warren, has argued that there are no errors to make in PROLOG. You can either omit some relevant piece of knowledge from the knowledge base or you can include some information which ought not to be there. Either way, the error (if we call it that) which shows up is that you will not get exactly the answers that you expected. Such errors are not 'system crashes' – it is natural that some questions have no answers from a given knowledge base.

There are problems. In particular we still find it difficult to deal with explicitly negative information. Harnessing the full power of predicate logic is not at present within our grasp, and in using PROLOG we have to accept the limitations of the Horn clause subset of full first-order logic. Our objective remains full logic programming, and we are constantly surprised by what can be achieved with the tools currently at our disposal. Our work which children, for instance, indicates that the availability of logic as a computer language can provide a considerable enhancement to the learning, not only of logic, but of the whole range of school subjects, where there is an agreed emphasis on the value of developing logical thinking.

5.2 HARNESSING THE SKILLS AND ENTHUSIASMS OF TRAINED MINDS

Current implementations of PROLOG are crude and limited relative to the aspiration of full logic programming, but even so we can make use of it as a tool in a range of intellectual activities. Whereas ten years ago possible users were put off by the cost of the computer hardware and PROLOG implementations were hard to obtain, neither of these problems remains, and considerable research effort has been devoted to improving the user-friendliness of available systems. Indeed, among the objectives of the Japanese Fifth Generation Project is the development of 'handy' systems that are amenable to use by the non-computer-specialist, ideally in his or her natural language. Our work at Imperial College on the project 'Logic as a computer language for children' should be seen in this context. Schools provide a ready captive source of non-computer-specialists, in a context where intelligent learning is the objective. We have been able both to develop materials for teaching Logic as a Computer Language in its own right, and to work with subject specialists in developing materials to assist in the teaching of a wide range of school subjects. This experience has also been used for work with other non-computer-specialists such as historians, doctors, linguists, and social scientists, drawing on the expertise of trained minds in their own areas of specialist interest. Logic can offer a common notation, and a declarative approach to logic programming can prove extremely useful, not so much in providing 'all the answers' but in focusing attention on a new series of interesting questions.

With the recent proliferation of relevant software it has been important to adopt an approach that is as far as possible independent of particular machines, implementations, or even of a particular language. It was gratifying to establish, on a recent visit to Syracuse, a common context with researchers using the logic programming language LOGLISP, and to see them making imaginative use of micro-PROLOG, while also working on a new PROLOG implementation making use of meta-language for large-scale applications. A particular research product of 'Logic as a Computer Language for Children' has been the 'Simple' front-end program, making the language more accessible to naive users. Similar front-end programs are now also becoming available for other implementations, and the exercises developed with children and described in *Beginning micro-PROLOG* can be used with many different machines, implementations, and languages.

An overview of programming activities in the current logic programming community would indicate the evolution of a number of different styles. In particular Clocksin & Mellish, in their "Programming in PROLOG" (1981), have emphasized the power of PROLOG as a programming language like many others, with a procedural approach and concern for efficiency. The wide range of practical applications of PROLOG in Hungary described by Szeredi and his colleagues have incorporated the use of other languages and non-logical augmentations to PROLOG. Kowalski and the Imperial College Programming Group have concentrated on the declarative style, sacrificing considerations of efficiency on current single-processor backtracking implementations in favour of exploring in more theoretical terms the power of logic, and implementations on new machines with parallel architecture, being built at Imperial College and elsewhere. Interestingly, different groups of Japanese researchers are following analogous research strategies, developing both parallel implementations of PROLOG and 'hybrid' systems incorporating elements of PROLOG, LISP, and SMALLTALK.

Our work with children and non-specialists has been predominantly declarative. We have placed considerable emphasis on clear description and the development of correct specifications, placing an intitial onus on the clear thinking of the subject specialist. The description provides us with a program capable of a wide range of possible uses.

Many long words in English are made up of several components, so that it is possible to make sense of an unfamiliar word by breaking it down into familiar parts, and assembling the meanings of the parts into some impression of the meaning of the whole word. A large number of such words are based on Latin, and have a number of common prefixes such as

prefix (extra)
prefix (super)
prefix (in)
prefix (con)
prefix (manu)
prefix (trans)

common stems, such as

stem (marit)
stem (natur)
stem (dur)
stem (fac)

and suffixes, such as

    suffix (al)
    suffix (ing)
    suffix (ally)
    suffix (ture)

We can give simple meanings for each of these components, as follows:

extra	means	beyond
super	means	more-than
in	means	in
con	means	together
manu	means	with-hands
trans	means	across
marit	means	wedlock
natur	means	life
dur	means	hard
fac	means	make
al	means	(adjective use)
ing	means	(present-participle use)
ally	means	(adverb use)
ture	means	(noun use)

Our program merely consists of the vocabulary and meanings described above, together with list-processing programs that decompose compound words and assemble the meanings of their components, as listed below:

x has-meaning (y z X) if x decomposes-to (Y Z x1) and
                    Y   means y and
                    Z   means z and
                    x1 means X

[This sentence can be read in English as

"A compound word x has the composite meaning (y z X) if it can be decomposed into three parts, Y Z and x1, which have the respective meanings y, z and X."

Note that at this stage we do not know how to decompose a compound word. That is to be defined later.]

x decomposes-to (y z K) if prefix (y) and
                           stem (z) and
                           suffix (X) and
                           Y STRINGOF y and
                           Z STRINGOF z and
                           x1 STRINGOF X and
                           APPEND (Y Z y1) and
                           APPEND (y1 x1 z1) and
                           z1 STRINGOF x

[This sentence can be read in English as

'A compound word x can be decomposed into three parts (y z X) if y is a prefix, z is a stem and X is a suffix, and if when the letters of y, z and X are put together they make up the letters of x.'

STRINGOF is a built-in PROLOG program that describes the relation between words and the list of characters from which they are formed.
APPEND is a PROLOG program that describes the relation between two lists and the list that is produced if they are put together (or appended).]

We have not decided in advance how our description is to be used, what should be 'inputs' and what should be 'outputs'. That is for the computer system to determine in the light of questions that we may ask.

We now have a flexible system available, which can be used in a number of different ways. We can find out the meaning of a word.

which (x: manufacture has-meaning x)
            (with-hands make (noun use))
No (more) answers

We can generate a set of words, many of them new to the English language, on a particular theme.

which (x y:x has-meaning (y wedlock (adjective use)))
            extramarital beyond
            supermarital more-than
            inmarital in
            conmarital together
            manumarital with-hands
            transmarital across
No (more) answers

We can also generate a large dictionary of compound words, together with their overall meaning, by asking

which (x y : x has-meaning y)
            extramarital (beyond wedlock (adjective use))
            extramariting (beyond wedlock (present-participle use))
            extramaritally (beyond wedlock (adverb use))
            supermarital (more-than wedlock (adjective use))
            supermariting (more-than wedlock (present-participle use))
    etc

The program can obviously be extended by increasing the number of prefixes, stems, and suffixes, which will broaden the range of words produced but render the response time progressively slower. This program deals with a subset of Latin derivatives, and a super-set of compound words in general use from such roots. Equivalent programs could easily be written to handle words derived from the Greek, and for handling words in modern languages such as

German that are built up in an analogous manner. The simple grammatical information provided by the suffix could prove useful as a link to a more general parsing program, giving clues regarding the semantics of a word and thus the sentence under analysis. At present the program is merely an automated version of word analysis in terms of prefix, stem, and suffix, as provided in beloved classroom texts such as Kennedy's *Latin primer.*

Work with subject specialists can place the computer scientist in the role of consultant. A subject specialist such as a history teacher may wish to specify the desired format of answer patterns in classroom interactions, and may become involved in broader issues of design of the man—machine interface. Research in such issues is considering intelligent means of displaying and manipulating information on a screen, and the interactive use of PROLOG whereby the system can query the user in the same notation as is used by the user to query a database. The translation of sentences between two languages, for instance, can be facilitated by the system obtaining answers to questions from the user rather than requiring access to an enormous database of dictionary meanings and grammatical information.

This work places little emphasis on the PROLOG execution strategy and the exigencies of the single processor. Rather we have been concerned to take the user's description as it stands as a query or as an addition to a program. In our work with twelve-year-old children using census information from Wimbledon in 1871, they have been able to add their own definition of wealth in terms of the information available to them. They were each familiar with the census entries for a few individual residents of Church Street, and knew that there was no information recorded concerning salaries or incomes. They suggested that it would be useful to count the number of servants living at the same address as a Head of Household, and that this would indicate his wealth. Their rule was expressed as follows:

```
x wealth y if x relation Head and
             z isall (X : X relation Servant and
             x live-at Y and
             X live-at Y) and
             z length y
```

A more sophisticated system, such as Warren and Pereira's (1981) 'Chat 80' would re-order the conditions of that rule to enhance the efficiency of its use. Our concern was that a correct description should lead to correct answers to appropriately expressed questions.

Even such small-scale work using logic and programming has raised interesting issues for those concerned with 'mind and machine'. Our toy example of an expert system for finding faults in bicycles can spark off discussions of the nature of expertise. We can describe the causes of various faults that have been observed to occur:

```
puncture causes flat
leaky-value causes flat
```

```
flat causes uneven-ride
broken-spoke causes distorted-wheel
distorted-wheel causes uneven-ride
distorted-wheel causes erratic-braking
broken-cable causes brake-failure
brake-failure causes accident
```

We can add a rule that tells us that one thing can lead to another, that one fault can lead to a chain of consequences for the complex system that is your bicycle.

```
x leads-to y if x causes y
x leads-to y if x causes z and
                z leads-to y
```

Given an observed problem of an uneven ride, we can trace its origins.

```
which (x : x  leads-to uneven-ride)
            flat
            distorted-wheel
            puncture
            leaky-valve
            broken-spoke
No (more) answers
```

Alternatively, we can explore the consequences of an observed fault such as a broken spoke.

```
which (x: broken-spoke leads-to x)
          distorted-wheel
          uneven-ride
          erratic-braking
No (more) answers
```

On a larger scale we will be concerned with more complex information, and with expressing probabilities or degrees of certainty, but the same simple principles will apply.

By taking small examples of complex issues we can often establish common ground between practitioners of what had appeared to be radically different disciplines. The bicycle example, for instance, can strike familiar chords in the minds of doctors, engineers, historians, musicians, linguists: and the common notation and computer assistance are available to all. A simple logic program can prove to be a powerful heuristic tool. Our example is taken from economics, where the concern is to develop deductive systems based on *a priori* premises. The method consists of selecting appropriate entities, specifying the environment in which they interact, and setting them up in a model in which their interactions are worked out by mathematical logic. Our particular subject is economic policy, and we are exploring the consequences of a policy of deflation. A static account of policies and their consequences appears non-controversial:

deflation means raise-taxes
raise-taxes means lower-spending-power
lower-spending-power means lower-demand-for-products
lower-demand-for-products means less-demand-for-imported-finished-products
lower-demand-for-products means less-demand-for-imported-inputs-for-
    manufacture
lower-demand-for-products means lower-investment
less-demand-for-imported-finished-products means balance-of-payments-more-
    favourable
less-demand-for-imported-inputs-for-manufacture means balance-of-payments-
    more-favourable
lower-investment means lower-productivity
lower-productivity means less-competitiveness
less-competitiveness means balance-of-payments-less-favourable
less-competitiveness means unempolyment
unemployment means lower-spending-power

As with the bicycle example, we can add rules describing how one thing can lead
directly or indirectly imply another:

    x implies y if x means y
    x implies y if x means z and
              z implies y

We can recursively construct a chain of connections for such a model:

    (x y) chain ( ) if x means y
    (x y) chain (z : X) if x means z and
               (z y) chain X

The dynamic power of this model greatly exceeds appearances. If we ask, for
instance, what is implied by a policy of deflation

    which (x:deflation implies x)

we receive as answers a non-terminating list of consequences, demonstrating the
'vicious circle' of deflation resulting from increasing unemployment on this
model. On the computer we can break out by using 'Control C', but in reality
some correcting action is required; if, that is, we accept the premises of the
argument. The same program will generate an infinite set of connections between
deflation and unempolyment in answer to the question

    which (x:(deflation unemployment) chain x)

    The approach of logic programming as described depends fundamentally
on a view of problem solving as problem decomposition. Further issues remain
concerning knowledge representation, for although predicate calculus is an
appropriate notation, there remains the problem of the initial abstraction that
accompanies even the object level of description. Experimental work with
children developing their own programming projects has emphasized the impor-

tance of this stage. Children who are successful at the whole range of programming exercises remain uncertain about the first move to a choice of representation. We should not be surprised at this difficulty: as Hoare wrote in his *Notes on data structure:* "In practice, even in the formulation of a problem, the programmer must have some intuition about the possibility of a solution; while he is designing his abstract program, he must have some feeling that an adequately efficient representation is available". Such intuitive feels cannot be relied on in the non-specialist. The research of the author is concerned with this problem and some answers appear to be available in the work of structuralist social scientists and philosophers, where a different view is taken of the distinction between problem solving and knowledge representation. The mode of description of a particular individual, and his actions or written products, cannot be considered separately from the context within which he is working, both intellectual and social. Correspondingly, preliminary research indicates that appropriate software tools for description and problem solving can be provided for practitioners of a particular discipline, given a knowledge of the discipline and of the previous work of the individual concerned, and making use of a combination of object level and meta-level reasoning within logic programs.

We are dealing here with complex issues. They are not new, but have troubled academics over the centuries working in a number of traditional disciplines. What is new is that we have discovered a way to begin to harness the power of computer technology to the ancient chariot of logical thinking. There is a fresh stimulus to unearth the work of past charioteers, and to combine the resources of the range of the world's current intellectual 'gymnasts', producing the 'chariots of fire' of the new generation.

An earlier version of this chapter was presented as a paper with Jonathan Briggs of Imperial College at the 'mind and machine' conference in 1983 at Middlesex Polytechnic, and published in *The mind and the machine: philosophical aspects of Artificial Intelligence* edited by Steve Torrance, published by Ellis Horwood 1984.

6

Historical simulation and information retrieval

6.1 CLASSROOM HISTORICAL SIMULATION

An account is needed of how micro-PROLOG came to be applied to historical materials, and to simulations in particular.

My experience as a history teacher and head of a history department was that most of the published historical simulations did not seem very adaptable to my requirements. I was teaching classes of approximately thirty students, of varying academic ability, aged between eleven and sixteen. I wanted to create a classroom situation where each student was place in the position of decision-maker. Decisions should be made within the historical context as far as it could be reconstructed, without undue restrictions on the nature of decisions to be made, and with the facility for decisions to influence materially the subsequent progress of the simulation. This is in marked contradistinction to conventional historical simulation materials, where a linear progression and a predefined set of outcomes are common characteristics.

Why then involve the use of computers, full of unknown dangers for the unsuspecting historian? One impression I have formed of 'experience-centred' lessons is that, though involvement at the emotional level can be intense, the intellectual quality of the activity can be diminished by the lack of fine detail and by the enforced crudeness of some aspects of decision making based on incomplete information. My interest in involving computer technology in simulation has been in order to bridge the information gap, to provide information to classroom participants that will enable them to make coherent decisions within the historical context of the simulation. I have no interest in the computer as judge or arbiter, substituted for the toss of a coin or the roll of a dice, unless the basis for such judgment is specified in the historical evidence forming the framework of the simulation.

First attempts to develop materials along these lines were made at Sweyne

School in Essex, using BASIC, the most commonly available computer language for use with microcomputers in school. A working version of a simulation based on the Norman Conquest was produced and used in class, as well as being subjected to critical examination by the Schools Council Computers in the Curriculum History Project in 1979. The computer-aided simulation based on the Russian Revolution was produced for discussion with publishers in 1980.

There appeared, however, to be a number of crucial limitations that rendered the materials of doubtful value in rigorous history teaching. The data description in the database of information on individual characters was very limited, not reflecting the richness of detail that was wanted. The process of interrogating and updating the database was relatively elaborate and pre-set, with a finite range of queries and updatings available to the participants. The database operated independently of the chronological program that presented historical choices to be made; and the impact of decisions on the subsequent chronological program and state of the database was, though clear at certain times, cruder and more limited than was wanted. The course of the simulation was not linear, and did allow for the effects of decisions by a number of participants, but still the directions and guidance for participants were pre-set, albeit in a range of permutations. One was obliged to adopt representational and explanatory models that could be offered easily in BASIC. The historical problem had to be adapted to the needs of the computer formalism, and suffered from crudities and distortions in the process.

I would now like to outline the strategy adopted in using PROLOG as the language to handle one of the same historical simulations, working from identical historical source materials and accompanied by the same printed documentation. The initial example is a simple one.

Russian Revolution

The briefing information for individual characters for the 'Russian Revolution' game, as with other games I have produced, was written before the development of computer-assisted versions of the simulation materials. The model of constructing such briefings was of a network of relationships, a representation of the positions, wants, tactics, and problems of thirty historical characters in the 'action set', presented using a common vocabulary as far as possible for ease of developing and contrasting the information given. Participants should be able to function initially using the information given, but be equipped with the language, constructs, or notation with which to expand or change over the course of the simulation.

Translation of the individual briefing materials into a PROLOG database was extremely straightforward. As a test of the validity of such a translation, the original written briefings are still used, and are valuable for participants as a statement in natural language of their starting position. The PROLOG database has immediate advantages, for participants can ask questions, whose answers help them reach decisions. The questions are asked in PROLOG, and use the same formalism as the database. Participants can themselves amend the database, by deleting sentences, adding new sentences, or making changes using the editor.

To facilitate use of the database by students with little or no experience of PROLOG, it is constructed in a simple notation, largely made up of simple sentences whose interpretation in English is explicit. Economy of programming style can be sacrificed in the cause of participation. Here are some example sentences from the database:

Stalin member Bolsheviks
x wants revolution if x member Bolsheviks
Lenin tactics non-cooperation

Below are a few examples of questions:

English: Does Lenin support the Tsar?
PROLOG: is (Lenin supports Tsar)
               NO

English: Who has tactics of non-cooperation?
PROLOG: which (x:x tactics non-cooperation)
                   Lenin
               No (more) answers

To add new information, for example, regarding a Peasant, we can write

add (Peasant wants peace)

The revised database can be saved at any stage of the simulation, preferably with a series of different filenames to avoid loss of information that will prove valuable in the discussion that follows the simulation.

In a conventional simulation it is very important to establish the historical context, to reduce the level of anachronism and misconception. Often an introduction is provided, whether in the form of an opening lesson, a talk, film, or printed materials. Such an introduction will offer a framework, and begin to sketch in a background, upon which the simulation is to be constructed.

In the case of the 'Russian Revolution' simulation, printed introductory materials describing the state of Russia at the turn of the Twentieth Century, Russian involvement in the First World War, and social and political tensions, have normally been used, serving to provide a context for the events of 1917 that are to be reconstructed by the participants in the classroom.

A few names and details were discarded on reflection, but the framework was faithfully recorded. Students can still have the original printed versions, but the PROLOG programs can directly affect the other components of the 'Russian Revolution' package, written in the same notation with a common vocabulary.

For example, historical background information is represented:

(Russia mobilises army) date 1914

We can find out information about the different political parties:

English: What did the Bolsheviks want?
PROLOG: which (x:Bolsheviks want x)
                   abolish-property

                            income-tax
                            nationalise-industry
                            free-education
                            world-revolution
                            remove-bourgeoisie
                            dictatorship-of proletariat
                  No (more) answers

No amendment of these programs is necessary. They are designed to apply
constraints from the real world to the closed world of the simulation, in a way
that can visibly affect the logic of decision. One of our purposes in teaching
history is to enable our students to understand the reasons for action of historical
agents. One way towards this goal is to construct a practical inference, a reconstruction of the situation from the agent's point of view. The use of PROLOG
simulation programs would appear to hold considerable promise in this work of
modelling and reconstruction.

   It is crucial to the success of an historical simulation that events and decisions
can be located in a temporal context. To avoid needless anachronism one should
be able to establish what known historical events have preceded the situation
under reconstruction. Similarly, during the simulation, it is important to know
what 'holds true' at any given time and for participants to be able to record their
decisions and actions in the same notation, forming part of the framework for
later decisions.

   For instance, using a greatly simplified version of the program, we could say
that the Bolsheviks opposed the war for all twelve months of 1917:

   (Bolsheviks oppose war) for (1 12)

If we are now at month 3 in the simulation and want to know what is known to
hold true, we can ask:

   which (x:x at 3)
            (Bolsheviks oppose war)
   No (more) answers

We might want to record a decision of a participant at this stage:

   add ((Tsar visits army) at 3)

This is now added to the program recording what is known to hold true, so that
if we ask our question again, we get a new answer:

   which (x:x at 3)
            (Bolsheviks oppose war)
            (Tsar visits army)
   No (more) answers

   Finally we need to consider directions and guidance for participants during
the running of the simulation. The PROLOG notation is easily adapted to take
on the role of a simple 'expert system' in providing direction. Ant any given
stage, or 'round', the program can refer participants to particular primary or

secondary historical sources, can emphasize particular instructions, or perhaps set particular questions or problems to participants. This program is designed to be amended by the teacher as required, to take account of the needs of his particular students.

For instance, if we have reached month, or round, 5, we can type in:

add (game round 5)

To find out what the key issue is thought to be, we can ask:

which (x: issue now x)
        reforms
No (more) answers

To find out which of the printed documents to refer to at this stage, we can ask:

which (x: see source x)
        (24 25 26)
No (more) answers

It will be noted that in **PROLOG** simulations as described, the computer is not presented as decision-maker or arbiter. Rather it is used to facilitate judgement and decision on the part of the students, to extend their capacity to consider information and see the effect of their decisions and actions on the network of which they form part. The example described above has been used both as a classroom simulation as originally intended, and as an introduction to PROLOG which can then be used for numerous other applications in the field of history teaching and elsewhere.

European Parliament

A more complex example of this approach to computer-aided simulation concerned the European Parliament. A modern history class was studying the development of the European Economic Community, with different students researching the different member countries and institutions, as well as the political parties. Information was obtained from the European Commission and from the political parties compaigning for support in the European elections. Each student developed knowledge of their own specialist area in preparation for a mock 'European Parliament' where they would speak on behalf of the country, institution or party they had researched.

In order to make a useful contribution to the debate the students needed information about the position of other participants — their wealth, their policies, their problems, the political strength of different parties. In a debate where only information on paper was available, requests for information could be made but rarely satisfied. When the information was represented as a PROLOG database, the description of the information required was a question to the database.

The program was written in a modular manner, so that sections could be interrogated separately or together. Here are some example questions, in English and PROLOG:

What is the population of Italy?
which (x: Italy population x)

How many MEP members does the United-Kingdom have?
which (x: United-Kingdom MEP-members x)

Why did France join the EEC?
which (x: France joined-for x)

What happened before the Treaty of Rome?
which (x: x before (Treaty of Rome))

What are the principles of the Socialists?
which (x: Socialists principle x)

In a particular debate use could be made of a policy modelling program, such as the economic modelling program described earlier. Rather than considering the effect of deflation according to the model purely in the abstract, it can be applied to the economy of a chosen country, such as the United Kingdom:

which (x y : deflation implies x and
              United-Kingdom GDP z and
              z changes-to y)

This question receives as response the succesive consequences of a deflationary policy and the resulting impact on the figure for the gross domestic product, using a simple 'multiplier' for each passage through the economic cycle.

Further extensions to the program can address particular issues such as the budget, defence, or the common agricultural policy. PROLOG can be used interactively to carry out opinion surveys and to help with the analysis of results.

Here the developing PROLOG program is a tool to aid historical inquiry in the classroom. It can aid simulation both of complex events and interrelations and of the process of questioning and reasoning needed to unravel them. This is perhaps reminiscent of Piaget's concern to unravel the complexity of the mollusc world in his work of classifcation for his doctorate, and his realization that a sequence of logical operations was required in order to attain understanding. Here we are regarding logic as a language, and using it as a tool in our quest for understanding.

6.2 PROLOG FOR INFORMATION RETRIEVAL

The other major area of application of computers in history teaching in England to date has been information retrieval. There has been a great deal of recent interest following Labbett's work in census data interrogation, and use of other primary sources of evidence.

I want to maintain that, except with very large databases, this work is most easily done using PROLOG.

Using the data printed in the Schools Council Project Paper 12 from the 1851 census in Dudley, we can represent the information as a **PROLOG** database preserving the original words and notation of the census enumerator, adding the relation 'person' and some brackets to impose form on the data. The information in the transcript is presented in tabular form, following a template:

place name relation condition age sex occupation birthplace

The form in which the information is represented in the PROLOG program is:

(place) person (name relation condition age sex occupation birthplace)

The program begins:

(47 Wordsley) person ((Jane Webb) Daughter ( ) 7 F (Scholar)
(Stafford Kingswinford))

(48 Wordsley) person ((William Leck) Head M 56 Male (Gardener)
(Stafford Wolverhampton))

(48 Wordsley) person ((Elizabeth Leck) Wife M 51 F (Laundress)
(Stafford Wolverhampton))

We can add **PROLOG** sentences to retrieve the information, using column heading of the original transcript, giving easy access to information about age, occupation, sex, etc. of different people. For example, to retrieve information about the addresses of different people recorded in the census, we could add:

x address y if y person (x|z)

This sentence describes the pattern in which the relevant information is stored. In English we are saying that to find which people live at what addresses, we should look at the 'person' program, and pick out the individual on the left, and the first of the list on the right-hand side of the world 'person'. (In the notation (x|z), 'x' stands for the first member of the list, the name, and 'z' represents the remainder of the list.)

English: What are the names of men who are heads of their households?

PROLOG: which (x:x sex Male and
                    x relation Head)

            (William Leck)
            (Richard Truman)
            (Benjamin Poyner)
         No (more) answers

English: What were the occupations of men aged over 20, but still unmarried?

PROLOG: which (x occupation y:x sex Male and
                    x age z and
                    20 LESS z and
                    x condition Un and

x occupation y)
(William Oldfield) occupation (Iron Moulder)
(Joseph Poyner) occupation (Glassmaker)
No (more) answers

There is no difficulty in constructing such a program. Recently in a Wimbledon school a class was working on the 1871 census for their area. They worked in groups transcribing from the census, finishing on a Tuesday, and used the completed program in class on the Friday.

The language is sufficiently simple for students to add to programs during a lesson. For example, a class of 12-year-olds decided to measure wealth in terms of the number of servants in the household of a head of household. One sentence of PROLOG was sufficient to implement this, and they could then obtain a list of householders and their wealth, together with occupation if desired. They then chose to investigate further one man who had a servant but no occupation. One question extracted the information that the man was born in Prussia, but had claimed to be a "naturalized British subject". Some students suspected the man of being a spy, and wanted to try to find out more about him from other documentary sources. Another man, by profession "Drill Sergeant of the 11th SRU and Pensioner of the Chelsea Hospital", had a servant with the same surname, which prompted further study of the system of servants in nineteenth century households.

The interrogation of the census data raised a number of historical issues to be explored with the help of further evidence. On this occasion the issues included: rates of pay for different occupations, social class differences linked to occupations, how servants could be related to their employers, relations between England and Prussia, and why servants had travelled from all over the country to work in Wimbledon. Hypotheses could be formulated, as with the definition of wealth, and test with the available evidence. Our wealth definition was clearly too simple, and would also tell us very little about an area like Dudley, where there were very few domestic servants. It did, however, give us some impression of social stratification in Wimbledon, where rich families had as many as nine servants, but lived next door to grooms and labourers.

A similar approach can be adopted with any information of a consistent form. Teachers who want their students to have access to tables of factual reference information to use when relevant, may like to have such information represented as a program. In this way, for instance, chronological date charts, often to be found at the back of history textbooks, can be made available. I have information about twentieth century America, Western Europe, and the Soviet Union available as three programs using the same names of relationships, and they can be consulted singly or in combination depending on the question that needs answering. For example, to find out what events are recorded as happening in the USA between 1930 and 1935, and in what years, we could ask:

which (x year y: (x date y) in USA and 1929 LESS y and y LESS 1936)

As all of the information in these programs is entered in the form:

('event' date 'year') in 'country'

it is not difficult to ask questions describing the information required.

Many other kinds of historical information come to us in a form that is amenable to representation as PROLOG programs. Henry Mayhew's monumental nineteenth century work *London labour and the London poor*, contains numerous tables of information derived from extensive research. One table, for instance, describes the amount of soot collected per week in different London parishes, and the number of master sweepers and journymen employed by each parish in busy and slack seasons. One group decided to compare the productivity of the different parishes, defining productivity as the amount of soot divided by the number of master sweepers. This produced a wide range of results, and prompted further enquires. On examining the employment practices of different parishes it was clear that some employed large numbers of journeymen, and others hardly any at all. It was not even clear that the distinction between masters and journeymen was consistently drawn. If we tried an alternative definition of productivity as the amount of soot divided by the number of masters and journeymen employed in the busy season, then we found that each parish had about the same result. By 'squeezing' the evidence, in Labbett's terms, we could answer some questions and raise many more. The capacity to add hypotheses and further information to the program is crucial here. Mayhew's research on levels of illness in different parts of London, where nearness to the river and height above water level can be relevant, is amenable to this kind of hypothesis testing. A wealth of research has been carried out, and tends to sit gathering dust on the shelves. We can re-inject life into that research, and evaluate different research findings in the classroom, with the aid of logic and the computer.

At the administrative and reference level the computer has much to offer. I like to build up programs of bibliographic references, so that when a student asks for books about Hitler, or a colleague asks for books or articles about simulations in history teaching, I can ask appropriate questions and provide printed answers from the computer. Stock records of books can be kept, and much of the information from reference books can be made more available in the form of programs. Tables of information encountered in, for instance, a course in social and economic history, can be represented as individual programs or combined in a cumulative database, extremely useful for hypothesis testing.

The above examples are early products of research using techniques of logic programming. Work is now proceeding on the representation of pieces of legislation as programs, on understanding natural languages such as English, and on representing the belief systems of the protagonists in, for instance, the current nuclear debate.

The Earls Colne project, based in the Department of Social Anthropology in Cambridge, has been working on the problem of community studies and individual reconstitution. It has been concerned with the collection and examination of written records involving a particular village. From these it is hoped to piece together a detailed view of the lives of the inhabitants over a three-hundred-year period. To this end approximately 1000 different sources have been collected about the village of Earls Colne, in Essex. These documents contain in total an estimated twelve million English words, which have been transcribed and typed into the computer.

The scale of the project is beyond PROLOG in its present implementations, and the Cambridge team have developed a relational database management system for this particular application, and a query language to search the records. Considerable advances have been made, in computing terms, with a parsing program that takes original historical text with no omissions and the addition of annotations into a semantic network capable of manipulation in the relational database (CODD) through the associated query language (CHIPS). This software has taken some years to develop, but has so far been used for very limited actual querying. Part of this limitation is due to the need of the computer scientists to have a prior clear idea of the kind of queries that are to be made, while the historian's perception of relevant queries develops with his actual involvement in handling the historical information. There is also the problem of record linkage, and little was known about the way in which pieces of information from such a wide range of documents would overlap and complement one another. King states that

> "The eventual aim of the project was to convert the semantic structure into a constructed 'historical' model, where the life histories of individuals could be examined and compared."

It would seem that PROLOG could have a number of possible advantages for future contributions to such a data-handling problem:

(1) The ease of interrogation of a logic database, without the need for a separate query language.
(2) The avoidance of a need for predetermination of queries for computer programmers to pre-process.
(3) The possibility in PROLOG of designing a parsing program that produces a more tractable database, while still retaining the original text from historical documents.
(4) The ease of data handling in PROLOG for the non-computer specialist. Relations can be defined in ordinary language that aids the retrieval of information in the way that the expert (historian) wants.
(5) PROLOG's attributes as an Artificial Intelligence tool. In a sense what is being modelled in such a project is the method and conclusions of the expert historian: success could be in the form of the expert (in this research project Sarah Harrison, who performed the parallel manual data processing) accepting the work of the computer system.
(6) PROLOG's developing features in terms of expert systems applications, and uses in belief systems and information systems modelling, seem appropriate. For instance, King was wanting to assign degrees of certainty to conclusions reached regarding the identities of individuals in Earl Colne, but was impos-

ing a system of weighting extraneous to the system or the programs currently developed. This could be improved.

(7) The transferability of the logic programming methodology. If one can handle the kind of documents involved in this problem, a range of official and other documents should become accessible to information retrieval after appropriate parsing.

7

Representing the knowledge of the expert archaeologist

The field of archaeology is now so extensive that no one individual can have complete knowledge of even one specialist area of work. Each researcher or enthusiast is dependent on the report and publications of fieldworkers, which will be subjected to the critical scrutiny of their academic peers prior to acceptance as reputable works for reference. The literature proliferates, often in a form not immediately usuable by the subsequent enthusiast.

7.1 HOW SHOULD AN ARCHAEOLOGIST PRESENT HIS EXPERTISE?

A number of problems lie behind this state of affairs, it is not generally agreed what an archaeologist is to do when he commits his expertise to paper. Is he to present a glorious catalogue of finds in the manner of Schliemann, a selective piece of autobiography following Howard Carter, another in one of the many series of introductions or field guides, a methodology of fieldwork in the style of Mortimer Wheeler, or simply a readable account, accessible to the layman, of the past history of a particular monument? Not only do we have to assess the nature of the expertise to be represented on paper or in some other medium, but the audience to which this expertise is to be communicated. There is a great difference between the form and purpose of a learned paper, and of a descriptive leaflet at an ancient monument.

It is arguable that conventional modes of publication are no longer adequate to satisfy the demand for the expertise of the archaeologist. The purpose of this chapter is to suggest some alternative approaches, and to concentrate particularly on the contribution to be made by logic programming and the development of expert systems.

7.2 WHAT IS AN EXPERT?

What does someone look for when consulting an expert? Hawkins, in his *An analysis of expert thinking* (Hawkins, 1981) says:

> "someone who can negotiate an agreed interpretation of a particular subject with the help of special knowledge and user opinions".

He adds that:

> "an expert appears very much as an analytical tool, helping the users make well-informed decisions without forcing them to accept any particular interpretation or procedure."

We are concerned in this chapter with two different kinds of consultation of an expert: by the interested layman and by the specialist in a related subject domain. In the first case the questionner wants an answer in ordinary language. In the second case the questionner wants to be able to communicate with other specialists and their areas of knowledge without being obliged to learn each other's specialized language and knowledge, through the medium of the expert.

7.3 ARTIFICIAL INTELLIGENCE AND KNOWLEDGE REPRESENTATION

Doran approached the problem of 'knowledge representation for archaeological inference' (Doran, 1977) ". . . in the light of the evolving artificial intelligence theories of specialist knowledge representation." We would agree with him that "archaeology has clear attractions as a problem-domain for artificial intelligence research", but would wish to recommend a different approach to the problem, arising from research in logic programming.

There has been a division in the AI community over the appropriate form for representing knowledge. As Mylopoulos says in his review of the area (Mylopoulos, 1980):

> "the current design paradigm for 'intelligent systems' stresses the need for expert knowledge in the system along with associated knowledge-handling facilities"

but:

> "the basic problem of knowledge representation is the development of a sufficiently precise notation for representing knowledge".

7.4 DECLARATIVE AND PROCEDURAL APPROACHES TO KNOWLEDGE REPRESENTATION

The fundamental division has been between the declarative and procedural approaches to knowledge representation. Doran's work falls into the procedural tradition, with knowledge conceived as a set of independent procedural or semi-procedural units. A similar approach would be to use "production rules", of the form:

"if A is encountered, then do X"

which is the approach of MYCIN (Shortliffe, 1978) and DENDRAL (Buchanan & Feigenbaum, 1978). Doran in his development of his system SOLCEM was more demanding, involving the use of a range of 'recognition demons' that correspond to concepts rather than broad sources of knowledge. Mylopoulos observes that procedural schemes of knowledge representation allow the specification of direct interactions between facts, thus eliminating the need for wasteful searching. However, he points out that it is difficult to understand and modify a procedural knowledge base.

By contrast, Mylopoulos emphasizes the simplicity of notation of a declarative logical representation scheme, which leads to understandable descriptions and conceptual economy. On this approach a knowledge base is a collection of logical formulae which provides a partial description of a subject domain. There are considerable advantages in using predicate logic as the notation for knowledge representation. Not least of these is the fact that, following Kowalski's suggestion (Kowalski, 1974) of the procedural interpretation of sentences of logic for problem solving, the language of PROLOG has developed in which statements of declarative description can also be given a procedural semantics. More recently Clark, Hammond, and McCabe have suggested that PROLOG is a suitable language for implementing expert systems (Hammond, 1980, 1983; Clark, McCabe & Hammond, 1981). It is from this standpoint that we approach the problem of archaeological knowledge.

7.5 THE NATURE OF ARCHAEOLOGICAL KNOWLEDGE

Before proceeding to the representation of archaeological knowledge we have to analyse its nature. Collingwood's remarks on the incomplete nature of the discipline of history also still holds true for archaeology:

> "the modern conception (of history) as a study at once critical and constructive, whose field is the human past in its entirety, and whose method is the reconstruction of that past from documents written and unwritten, critically analysed and interpreted, was not established until the nineteenth century, and is even yet not fully worked out in all its implications." (Collingwood, 1946.)

Daniel reminds us (Daniel, 1981) that:

> "our present state of knowledge is merely, like the present, a moment in time."

Daniel maintains that the links with scientists and scientific techniques dates from the beginning of this century:

> "By the outbreak of the war (1914) it was clear that archaeology as it developed was going to rely more and more on scientific techniques and was no longer the study of artefacts in the field and in museums in isolation.

> The archaeologist was becoming dependent on scientists who studied the flora, fauna and environment of his sites and who would date his material independent of archaeological methods." (Daniel 1981, p. 147).

Mortimer Wheeler accepted this scientific component of archaeological research, but wanted to emphasize that:

> "In a simple, direct sense, archaeology is a science that must be lived, must be 'seasoned with humanity'." (Wheeler, 1943.)

Within the discipline of archaeology we can discern different kinds of knowledge. As Elias writes in his *Sociology of knowledge* within such an activity:

> "Not only knowledge of objects, but also knowledge of how to gain and how to advance knowledge of objects, how to cath them in one's net, and how to make nets, and how to make better nets, for catching them, develops over the generations." (Elias, 1971, p. 166.)

We must not think that 'knowledge' is to be reduced to tabular data of some absolute kind. Cicourel observes:

> "The actual analysis of tabulated data. . . is dependent upon implicit theoretical and substantive knowledge obtained under considerably less rigorous conditions that knoweldge evident in the elegant tables presented." (Cicourel 1964, p. 108.)

It would be inappropriate to subdivide the task of archaeology into independent sub-tasks, for every act of archaeological interpretation is influenced by the results of every other act. Of course, however, archaeologists themselves simplify: the subject is broken down into specialist areas according to region or period or type of evidence. There will be factual knowledge that is particular to the specific domain, factual knowledge of the general subject area, knowledge of the procedures of the archaeologists, and general world knowledge deriving from the society and rationality within which he operates.

This amalgam of kinds of knowledge constitutes the expertise of the skilled practitioner, which is to be represented by our system. This assumes the existence of a unified activity or form of knowledge. The intention is that this should be modelled by a program, using the knowledge of an individual expert consultant, refining the model to generate correct output consistent with answers that would be given by the expert consultant himself.

7.6 CONSULTATION BY THE INTERESTED LAYMAN

Our first example application of this approach to knowledge representation would be analogous to the introductory textbooks, field guide, or descriptive document available at museums and ancient monuments.

It could be argued that this was an appropriate area for an expert system on a number of grounds. There is a need to preserve the knowledge of expert curators whose services are being dispensed with as the Department of the Environment seeks economies and privatization. The cost of microcomputers is falling while the level of public interest in archaeology is ever-increasing. Laymen need an introduction to diverse sources of information, either in a formal classroom situation or in the form of references and information when interest has been aroused in a particular subject.

This example program uses micro-PROLOG with the SIMPLE front-end program. The source of information was Wood's field guide "Archaeology in Britain" (Wood, 1979). The text can easily be represented in predicate logic in the micro-PROLOG form. Early on, abbreviations are provided for county names:

(Bedfordshire)	abbrev Bd
(Berkshire)	abbrev Bk
(Buckinghamshire)	abbrev Bc
(Cheshire)	abbrev Ch

Wood develops a glossary of useful technical terms:

(Barrow)	gloss	(mound covering a burial)
(Beaker people)	gloss	(first Bronze Age immigrants)
(Bell pit)	gloss	(pit for extraction of clay for iron-making)

He offers some generalizations regarding patterns of settlement:

x live   ((Thames Valley)) if
                x period (early Palaeolithic)
x live   ((NE Wales) (Derbyshire) (Yorkshire) (E Coast)) if
                x period (later Palaeolithic)

Most interesting perhaps is his section entitled 'Identifying earthworks' (p. 77). His account takes the form of a series of rules, each of the form:

If you see . . . it could be . . . For more detail, see Page . . .

To enhance the compactness of the rules, further abbreviations are given, which we represent as:

N	date	((neolithic)	(−4000	−2400))
B	date	((Bronze Age)	(−2400	−700))
E	date	((early)	(−2400	−1500))
M	date	((middle)	(−1500	−1000))
L	date	((late)	(−1000	−700))
I	date	((Iron Age)	(−700	50))
R	date	((Roman)	(50	400))
D	date	((Dark Age)	(400	650))
S	date	((Anglo-Saxon)	(500	1100))
Med	date	((medieval)	(1100	1500))
Mod	date	((modern)	(1500	2000))

Using Wood's form above, some rules could be represented as follows:

(low small round mound) could-be ((S Barrow) 154))

[If you see a low small round mound, it could be an Anglo-Saxon Barrow, for more detail see page 154]

(group of low round or oval mounds) could-be ((S Cemetery) 155))

[If you see a group of low round or oval mounds, it could be an Anglo-Saxon Cemetery, for more detail see page 155]

(conical mound often with flat top) could-be ((R Barrow) 153))

[If you see a conical mound, often with a flat top, it could be Roman Barrow, for more detail see page 153]

If we want to identify the possible period of some earthwork we have seen, we can use the rule:

x possible-period y if x could-be ((z X) Y) and
z date y

To pick out what type of earthwork we have seen, we can use the rule:

x type y if x could-be ((z y) X)

To get direct access to the relevant page numbers, we can use the rule:

x described-on-page y if x could-be (z y)

This information can be presented to the user in the form of a system that will identify a given earthwork, with the program questionning the user where further details are required to aid identification. A master program can call up and delete programs from disk as the interaction proceeds, making maximum use of core memory and of the facility for access to relations on disk.

Example questions
Let us illustrate how this fragment of the program will work by asking a number of questions.

English: What county is abbreviated as Bk?
PROLOG: which (x:x abbrev Bk)
(Berkshire)
No (more) answers

English: What does the glossary tell us about the Beaker people?
PROLOG: which (x: (Beaker people) gloss x)
(first Bronze Age immigrants)
No (more) answers

English: Tribe A was from the later Palaeolithic period.
Where could they have lived?
PROLOG: add (Tribe-A period (later Palaeolithic))
which (x: Tribe-A live y and
x ON y)
(NE Wales)

(Derbyshire)
(Yorkshire)
(E Coast)
No (more) answers

English: What earthworks are dealt with in the identification guide that mention a mound or mounds in the description?
PROLOG: which (x:x could-be y and
                         (either mound ON x
                            or mounds ON x))
            (low small round mound)
            (Conical mound often with flat top)
            (group of low round or oval mounds)
            No (more) answers

English: What period could the low small round mound date from?
PROLOG: which (x: (low small round mound) possible-period x)
            (500 1100)
            No (more) answers

English: What earthworks could be types of Barrow?
PROLOG: which (x:x type Barrow)
            (low small round mound)
            (conical mound often with flat top)
            No (more) answers

English: From what periods could types of Barrow date?
PROLOG: which (x:y type Barrow and
                        y possible-period x)
            (500 1100)
            (50   400)
            No (more) answers

English: What is there of interest described on Page 153?
PROLOG: which (x:x described-on-page 153)
            (conical mound often with flat top)
            No (more) answers

7.7 ADVANTAGES OF A COMPUTER REPRESENTATION

You will note that the computer representation of the information offers a number of advantages over a conventional printed text.

(1) It can be asked questions, which may involve exploring information from a number of different parts of a book.

(2) Questions can be asked which were not envisaged when the information was entered.

(3) If we take advantage of the 'Query-the-User' facility (by using APES instead of SIMPLE when running the program) the system can prompt us for missing

information, and as a result can 'learn' new knowledge during the interaction. We could, for example, use a technical term in our question which the system did not recognize. It could ask for a 'gloss', and match components of that gloss to knowledge already held in the program. I could ask about 'body heaps', and supply the gloss that a 'body heap' was a 'mound covering a burial'. It could then regard 'body heap' as a synonym for 'Barrow'.

(4) The user can at any time add, amend, or delete information, whether in the form of facts or rules. The program acts as a framework or structure on which a body of knowledge can be built.

7.8 DRAWBACKS WITH THE COMPUTER REPRESENTATION

(1) In the form displayed above, the user needs to have some familiarity with the syntax of micro-PROLOG and SIMPLE. Here we have assembled the program from nothing: we could instead use a database query package, written in PROLOG, which took our questions in ordinary English, translated them into PROLOG, and answered them. Such packages have been written, for example, the Chat-80 system of Warren and Pereira (1981), but take up a considerable amount of space in the computer. Friendly facilities and intelligent behaviour from the computer reduce the space available for our programs, and on today's computers in educational use, this can be critical. They may also restrict the flexibility with which the user can interact with the program. Historians such as Jon Nichol and Jackie Dean are producing history teaching packages that protect the user from the details of logic and syntax. Typically they also involve some sacrifice in logical power and flexibility by being tailored for particular uses.

(2) The program is only as good as its weakest link — and that could be the original description of the archaeological or historical knowledge. When we write in English, or describe things conversationally, we are often less than completely clear, and our classifications can be somewhat arbitrary, hard to justify rigorously. We may fill in the backgound to a problem in such a way that our audience can follow our drift and form an impression of what we are trying to say. When we use logic, our descriptions need to be clear and unambiguous. The computer will not make logical errors: but we may inadvertently give it information that is ambiguous, inconsistent, or simply downright incorrect. The blame rests with the human author, who may find his confidence and self-esteem injured by the demands and incomprehension of the computer, which cannot work without him.

7.9 CONSULTATION BY THE SPECIALIST IN A RELATED SUBJECT DOMAIN

Hawkins (Hawkins, 1981) is particularly concerned with the role of an expert system in aiding communication between specialists, each with their own technical language. He sees as the objective:

"Each user experiences a simulation based on expert knowledge. A good simulation allows the expert to translate one user's hypothesis into results, expressed in another user's language. Such a translation exposes one specialist's opinion, via an expert's knowledge-based skill in simulation, to the scrutiny of another specialist."

If this works, then:

"without being obliged to learn each other's specialized language and knowledge, one user can communicate with another through the medium of the expert."

The approach depends upon a sophisticated model of the understanding of the questioner:

"The appropriate explanation would depend on the expert's assessment of what the questioner has failed to understand, i.e. the difference between the questioner's model and the expert's model."

The expert remains a tool:

"The expert's role is to assist one, or several, users to assemble mutually consistent models of the same geological object.

This kind of analysis could be applied to the construction of an account of what had happened to Tollund Man, found in a Danish peat bog. From the first discovery of the body by farm labourers, through the autopsy, the collection of archaeological evidence, the carbon-dating, the research into the customs of Germanic tribes, a number of specialists were involved in handling information with different technical terms, mediated by the expert archaeologists whose job it was to produce a coherent, consistent, overall account. There were limits to what was possible. As Daniel wrote (Daniel, 1981):

"How much a reflection on archaeology is it that we could reconstruct his last meal but of course will never know his name, why he was hanged, or his last thought."

On a small scale, Jon Nichol and Jackie Dean have used the computer with PROLOG to help in the teaching about Tollund Man and similar cases (Nichol & Dean, 1984). They have followed a similar approach to that adopted by the Schools Council History 13–16 Project in their *What is history?* pack for schools. Whereas the order of questions from students, in their roles as historians, is relatively predictable in the paper-based Schools Council approach, Nichol and Dean report an enormous variety of lines of questioning where the onus is on the students to uncover the information which can give rise to further questions.

On a larger scale, one could envisage a set of programs dealing with different areas of specialism, all available to users through a query system, able to respond with questions to each other or to the user where further information was needed to arive at a collaborative conclusion. Already we can begin to connect our micro-PROLOG query system, with its interactive facilities, to large relational databases and economic and statistical models. What will remain most important is having a clear idea of what one wants to ask, and knowing what would count as an answer.

An earlier version of this chapter was presented as a paper 'Representing the expert knowledge of the archaeologist' at the 1982 Conference on Computer Applications in Archaeology, at Birmingham University, with Derek Brough, of Imperial College.

8

Using micro-PROLOG for classroom historical research

8.1 INTRODUCTION

As part of the Local Studies course at Bishop Wand Church of England Secondary School in Sunbury, use is made in class of trade directories for the village from the nineteenth century, in conjunction with other local records such as the census records for particular streets. Part of the course is spent on fieldwork, with walks around the village looking at old building, studying inscriptions on tombstones in the churchyard, and comparing the present-day village with what is shown on a series of maps dating back two hundred years, written accounts since Saxon times, and archaeological evidence.

   The work described here involved the use of the trade directories for 1826, 1840, 1860, 1865, 1872, and 1876. Each separate directory was represented as a PROLOG database, and as many as three directories could be loaded into memory at once for simultaneous interrogation. Most classroom activity focused on the computer interrogation of the directories for 1826, 1840, and 1867, with all of the directories also available in printed form, laid out on large cards for each pair of students. The computer used was a Corona, an IBM-PC-compatible portable microcomputer, using a version of micro-PROLOG that addressed 128K of memory.

8.2 USE OF THE TRADE DIRECTORIES WITHOUT A COMPUTER

Below are the questions usually set to the students when the directories are used without computer assistance. They indicate the general approach taken on the course, largely developed by Mrs Elizabeth Hossain.

Trade directory entries

1826

1. Who was the vicar?
2. Which house in Sunbury is described as "That late possessed by the Earl Pomfret"?
3. How many times a day were letters sent to London?
4. How many public houses were there in Sunbury in 1826?
5. What would a tallow chandler sell? Why was his job important?
6. Make a list of the jobs and services carried out in Sunbury.
7. How frequent was the coach service to London from Sunbury?

1840

1. Louisa Ruff seems to have more than one job. One is post mistress. What are the others?
2. What does a farrier do? Why would this job be very important in nineteenth century Sunbury?
3. Is the coach service to London more or less frequent than it was in 1826?
4. Who would you go to if you wanted a straw hat made in 1840?
5. How many fishmongers were there in Sunbury?
6. Who was the governor of the workhouse?

1867

1. What new invention has arrived in Sunbury by 1867? How do you know?
2. How could you travel to London in 1868? How frequent was the service?

1872 and 1876

1. Look at the addresses given for William Allen, baker, Charles Collett, and William Thomas Collins and Son. What appears to have happened between 1872 and 1876?

From 1801 a census was taken of everyone living in England and Wales. The trade directory entries give the details for 1821, 1831, and 1861.

1821	1,700
1831	1,863
1861	2,332

Draw a graph to show these figures.

8.3 USE OF THE TRADE DIRECTORIES WITH A COMPUTER

The class, of 25 twelve-year-olds, had no previous experience of either the computer or the trade directories. Seven directories, each lengthy and printed in small type, could not usefully be interrogated without first requiring some familiarity with the historical context, apart from what had been acquired on the course to date. An examination was made of the directory for 1826. Initial questions asked, for written answer and discussion, were:

1.   What five things do you notice about the directory?

There were a variety of responses, such as:

> not many people
> not many different jobs
> the people have been split up and classified
> for each person we have the name and group
> for some people we have an address
> for some people we have a particular job, or trade
> not many women mentioned
> some of the jobs are not known today

2.   What different jobs did people do in 1826 in Sunbury?

Students first wrote down the different jobs by hand, and then saw how the same question could be asked to the computer, and answered fully in seconds. In PROLOG the question was

> which (x y:x lived 1826 and
>   x trade y)

3.   What were the names of the pubs and their landlords in 1826?

Again the answers could be found by hand from this, the smallest of the directories. In PROLOG, the question was

> which (x y:x lived 1826 and
>   x trade (publican) and
>   x address y)

The idea was thus introduced that the historian needs to decide what question to ask of his evidence. If he has only a small amount of evidence to deal with, he can probably search for the answer perfectly well himself. If, however, he is faced by a large amount of evidence, such as the seven trade directories, he may be well advised to take advantage of the assistance of the computer, which can carry out the search according to his description of the information that is required. A good historian knows what questions to ask, and what to do with the answers. He must not be the slave of the evidence in front of him. Trade directories were produced for a particular purpose, and much information about the village will not have been explicitly included. The task is to reconstruct something of life in nineteenth century Sunbury, including relating it to other knowledge we have at a local, regional, or national level concerning the same period.

There followed the suggestion of a wide range of possible reserach projects, to be carried out by individuals or small groups over the two weeks of the course unit. Suggestions included

> following an individual: such as John Baker, Dr Seaton
> following a family: such as Baker, Lambert, Broxholm, Bolt
> following a trade: such as sadler, wheelwright, publican, baker, beer retailer

following institutions: such as workhouse, private asylum, schools and academies

following addresses: such as Sunbury Lodge, and noting the increasingly full addresses given including street names

comparisons of, for example, 1826 and 1840; 1840 and 1867

evidence for the role of women

evidence for changing means of transport

evidence for increasing education

evidence for family businesses

evidence for the influence of the river and the country

changing trades and occupations

The method to be used by the students was that they should choose a topic, and write their chosen title, followed by a short outline of what they wanted to investigate. They should then write down in English the first question that they wanted to ask the computer, bearing in mind the kind of information that is contained in a trade directory. The teacher then put the question in PROLOG to the computer, and the student made a note of the answer received. He could then ask further questions arising from what he had learnt, following the same procedure. He also noted what information he would require from other sources, such as further details about particular families which might be found from the local census records. In some cases the student had relevant knowledge from other sources, and this should be incorporated in the written notes. For example, a student investigating the Baker family knew of a house in Sunbury with an inscription saying that Robert Eldridge Baker (mentioned in the directories) had built it.

After the investigation, the work could be presented in a number of forms, all drawing on the research, such as

diary (perhaps of Miss Broxholm, the doctor's daughter)

biography (perhaps of the grocer who became a schoolmaster)

family history (Baker by name and baker by trade)

comparative study

play

traveller's tale (told by a visitor at the Flower Pot Inn)

guide to Sunbury, accompanied by maps

8.4 THE PROLOG REPRESENTATIONS OF THE TRADE DIRECTORIES

A sentence in PROLOG is used to represent the information for each person. For example, to take the first entry in the 1826 directory, concerning **Wm Barclay esq**

lived-1826 ((Barclay Wm esq) (Upper Halliford) gandc ( ))

and for the publican of the Flower Pot Inn

lived-1826 ((Long John) (Flower Pot) pub (publican))

As observed by the students, we have information about a person's name, address, grouping, and trade. In the above sentences that information is presented in that order. In some cases no specific address or trade is given, in which cases I have used '( )', denoting the empty list of information. There are rules to give us access to these items of information:

> x address y if lived-1826 (x y z X)
> x class Gentry-and-Clergy if lived-1826 (x y gandc z)
> x trade y if lived 1826 (x z X y)
> x lived 1826 if lived-1826 (x y z X)

The same approach is used for the 1840 and 1867 etc. directories with the only change being in the number of the year used in the sentences and rules.

Example student questions in English and PROLOG
Which people were wheelwrights by trade, and when did they live?
which (x y:x trade (wheelwright) and x lived y)

Which people were publicans, and which pubs did they run?
which (x y:x trade (publican) and x address y)

Which people are mentioned in the directories for 1826, 1840 and 1867?
which (x:x lived 1826 and x lived 1840 and x lived 1867)

What were the addresses of the Gentry and Clergy who described themselves as 'esq?' (This question arose with a student who was concerned to find out who had carriages, and where they lived.)
which (x y:x class Gentry-and-Clergy and esq ON x and x address y)

What was the total number of people mentioned in 1867?
which (x:y isall (z:z lived 1867) and y length x)

What were all the different jobs done by people, not counting those with no stated job?
which (x:y trade x and not x EQ ( ))

What different trades did people have in 1840?
which (x y:x lived 1840 and x trade y)

Whose trade included being a baker, and when did they live?
which (x y z:x trade y and baker ON y and x lived z)

Give me information on everybody's trade and class.
which (x y z:x class y and x trade z)

Give me the address and trade of people whose address was stated to be in Sunbury in 1840.
which (x y z:x lived 1840 and x address y and Sunbury ON y and x trade z)

Tell me about the trades of individuals who lived in 1826 and 1840.
which (x y:x lived 1826 and x lived 1840 and x trade y)

Tell me about the names, addresses and trades of members of the Bishop family, and when they lived. (The same question was asked about the Burchetts, the Lamberts, the Bakers, the Giles and the Middletons.)
which (x y z X:x trade y and Bishop ON x and x address z and x lived X)

What work did women do? We defined new rules that would pick out cases of people described as 'Miss' or '(Mrs)' in the directories.

> x female-doing y if x trade y and Miss ON x
> x female-doing y if x trade y and (Mrs) ON x

We can now ask:
which (x y:x female-doing y)

What did the 'Professional Persons' do?
which (x y:x class Professional-Person and x trade y)

What were the names and addresses of the hairdressers, and in what years? (The same form of question was asked about grocers, plumbers, smiths and sadlers.)
which (x y z X:x trade y and hairdresser ON y and x and
x lived X)

Questions raised by the students, but not answerable from the trade directories alone, with or without PROLOG:

What is the origin of the name Burchett? (or Bishop)

Where the different people with the same surname Bishop (or Baker etc.) related and, if so, in what way?

How were inns in the nineteenth century different from today? Students noted that the Flower Pot was a staging post for coaches, and that seats could be booked at the other inns.

When did the centre of activity in Sunbury really move from the riverside to the other end of Green Street, nearer the railway, and why?

What happened to people who were too young or too poor to be mentioned in the trade directories?

What happened in the private asylum at Halliford House, and at the workhouse on Sunbury Common?

How did life in Sunbury change with the coming of the railway?

What did the Gentry do all the time, as they had no stated trades?

What was going on in all the different schools and academies that are mentioned? Should we be surpised that one of them was run by a former grocer?

Why was insurance suddenly such a significant form of employment in Sunbury?

To what extent was Sunbury a country village at the beginning of the century? How did this change?

What problems did the police sergeant have to deal with?

Why did station-masters but not engine-drivers live in Sunbury, or would the directory not mention employees, or people who travelled to work?

Where had the Gentry got their money?

Was there increasing military activity in the area? We read of a military college, and a number of naval officers are local residents.

What was the extent of the influence of the church in Sunbury? Were the people named in the directories elsewhere recorded as church members; Did support for particular churches come from particular social classes or trades? Was the church particularly active in educational, social or mission work?

What do we know about local and parliamentary politics in the area? Who had the right to vote?

Were most people in Sunbury born in the area, or had many moved in for work or other reasons?

What were the working conditions like in the local shops and businesses?

Did many local people work as servants for the local gentry?

8.5 CONCLUSION

The research reports produced by our twelve-year-old historical researchers will not necessarily be long or of lasting quality. They will, however, have experienced something of what it is to ask historical questions, and to make sense of the answers. There can be some division of labour with the computer: the student decides what questions to ask, and the computer performs the mechanical search for the answers. The ease of representing information in PROLOG in a form that remains comprehensible, and the capacity to ask and answer numerous different questions, makes it possible for each individual or group to pursue a separate line of inquiry if they wish. New facts and rules can be added at will: sections of trade directories could be interrogated together with census data or entries from the parish register.

In the lessons described above, questions were asked in English by the students, and translated into PROLOG by the teacher. More sophisticated query systems are under development that will assist the user to formulate a query using a series of menus to clarify the structure and vocabulary of the database. Already developed, though very demanding of computer memory space, are systems that will automatically translate questions from English in PROLOG and answer them efficiently.

We should note the methodological context of historical research through asking questions. Questions to a PROLOG database can only be answered from the closed world of information that it contains. Many questions will require further information if they are to be answered. The computer can have a powerful motivating effect on research and learning: hypotheses can be tested and improved, new areas of interest can be brought to light. There will always be more questions than answers, and the computer can help clarify which lines of inquiry are worth pursuing at a given time.

Earlier versions of this chapter have been published in *Education et Informatique* November 1984 (in French) and in *Teachers, Computers and the Classroom*, eds. Reid, J., Rushton, J., Manchester University Press, 1985.

9

Conceptual modelling in history teaching: revolutions

9.1 INTRODUCTION

One of the problems in teaching and learning modern political history is the proliferation of technical language, words with a particular meaning that have come into general use because of their explanatory power for specialists in the field. These same words can be a barrier to understanding for the uninitiated. One means of performing the initiation rites, admitting the student into the ranks of historians, is to have classroom discussions that make progressively greater use of the technical terminology, enabling the students to take it on as their own. Another method, which may flow from the first, is to give the students the capacity to build and manipulate their own models of complex problems and issues, using the technical concepts as building blocks.

A lower sixth form history class at Ricards Lodge High School for Girls in Merton, taught by the Head of Sixth Form, Mrs Inga Watson, had been studying and comparing different revolutions. In class discussion they were attempting to compare and contrast the American, French, Russian, and Chinese revolutions. Was there a common model that could be applied to each case? Bold hypotheses were put forward, and then modified for the particular cases. Different class members had specialized in the different revolutions, and at the time of the initial group discussion the class as a whole had not made a detailed study of the Russian Revolution. The class had a record for fluent group discussion that was not matched by the quality of their individual written work. Their GCE examination would require them to move from a broad generalization to a more detailed argued answer to questions, with points backed by evidence. They could made some critical analysis of different points of view, detecting bias and different interpretations, but found writing their own account much harder.

In the class discussion particular concepts were recurrent as they considered the four example revolutions:

overthrow
government
power
interest groups
rich and poor
middle class
outside influence
weak rule
difficult circumstances
war
political belief

9.2 THE USE OF COMPUTER MODELS

One way of exploring concepts and building explanatory structures is by using a computer. Many different approaches are possible. Below I describe how different models were demonstrated to the students, using an approach borrowed from 'adventure games', how they constructed their own descriptive accounts, and how tools were developed to enable students to construct 'revolutionary adventure games' exploring different strategies and decisions open to the historical agents.

The haunted house

The first simple models, running on a Sinclair Spectrum microcomputer using micro-PROLOG, were devised with Gareth Williams of Imperial College. It is common in adventure games to be exploring a haunted house. We can describe the links between different rooms:

bedroom 1 to bedroom 2
bedroom 2 to landing
bedroom 1 to landing
bedroom 3 to landing
landing to hall
library to hall
kitchen to hall
lounge to hall
hall to outside

and we can describe what is to be found in each room:

ghost in bedroom 1
vapire in bedroom 2
zombie in bedroom 3
vampire in bedroom 2
chest in bedroom 2
stairs in hall
portrait in hall

stairs in landing
corpse in library
books in library
food in kitchen
etc

We can describe how people get from place to place:

x goes-to y if x to y
x goes-to y if y to x

We can say that people can see things that are in the same room as they are:

x can-see y if x position z and y in z

Someone can move to an adjacent room:

x can-move-to y if x position z and z goes-to y

Further extensions to this simple framework can allow the user to choose where he wants to go in response to questions, and to take various actions such as picking things up, putting them down, or maybe asking them questions (for example, in the case of the chest in bedroom 2, the user may want to ask what is inside). At any stage the user can scrutinize the state of the model, and add or delete details to taste.

The class structure
In history we are concerned with structures: physical, institutional, and conceptual. Some of the above framework for moving around a building, between rooms, can be modified to help us consider, for example, social class structures or the party political spectrum. We can describe the routes between the classes:

aristocracy to royalty
bourgeoisie to aristocracy
proletariat to bourgeoisie
peasantry to bourgeoisie
peasantry to proletariat

Individuals can travel either way:

x linked-to y if x to y
x linked-to y if y to x

Social class can be defined in terms of occupation:

x class y if x job z and z classed-as y

Some example job classifications can be given:

x classed-as royalty if x ON (king queen prince)
x classed-as aristocracy if x ON (duke bishop earl abbot noble)
x classed-as bourgeoisie if x ON (doctor lawyer merchant landlord)

x classed-as proletariat if x ON (steelworker factoryworker miner soldier
sailor shopworker)
x classed-as peasantry if x ON (farmer fisherman peasant)

The system can ask a user for his job in order to classify him as to social class.
It can also show him his prospects for social mobility:

x could-move-to y if x class z and z linked-to y

Naturally in different social structures there will be additional barriers to
social mobility, of which we might choose to take account, such as income,
educational background, religion.

The party political structure
In a similar way we can construct a crude model of the party poltical spectrum:

socialist near communist
social-democrat near socialist
liberal near social-democrat
conservative near liberal
authoritarian near conservative

Again we can define the links as going both ways:

x close-to y if x near y
x close-to y if y near x

In simple terms, we can say that you support a party if you agree with all its
policies:

x supports-party y if y is-a party and x agrees-with y
x agrees-with y if (forall y policies z
then x accepts z)

Again, a dissatisfied party supporter can explore alternatives, and move to his
chosen new political home.

The class structure model and the party political model can be used simul-
taneously, enabling one to follow a number of different factors in an individual's
make-up, identifying the range of important elements which have not been
covered. Such models do not purport to be complete, but to aid and stimulate
thought, giving concrete form to abstract concepts.

9.3 USE OF THE COMPUTER BY THE STUDENTS

The above models were introduced and demonstrated to the class following their
concept-based discussion of the example revolutions. It was clear that an
account in terms of class was still unfamiliar to them, partly owing to their
lack of knowledge of the Russian Revolution. This in turn made it harder for
them to make many comparisons between the Russian and the Chinese revolutions. Indeed, some of the class were regarding the British Industrial Revolution
as directly comparable with the French and American Revolutions.

The students quickly grasped, however, at a descriptive level, what the computer models were doing. As members of a generation accustomed to computers, they soon saw that the computer did not have all the answers, but would reflect the knowledge and understanding that they could bring to it.

The point of demonstrating the models was not that any particular model of explanation should thereby be adopted, but to illustrate how even a simple model could clarify complex issues. It would of course be preferable for the class to arrive at a model or models of their own. The objective was not the construction of models, but aiding in the construction of written explanations of historical problems, such as those set by examiners.

The next session was held in the school computer room, and the students made use of six microcomputers, both Research Machines and Sinclair Spectrums, to write their own first programs. The lesson started with a class discussion, going over similar ground to the previous discussion, but with more factual knowledge acquired in the interim. As an illustration of the descriptive use of PROLOG, I took notes of the discussion on the computer, picking out what were regarded as important causes of revolutions, difficulties in their leadership, and problems after taking control.

In their programs, the students concentrated on the countries they knew best, trying to identify the key information to give to the computer. Driven by content with which they were familiar, they had little difficulty with the 'SIMPLE' surface syntax of PROLOG, quite happy to ask complex queries, to use rules, and to structure their information into lists when the subject required it. After the first few sentences, the principal source of reference was their history notebook, where their notes tended to be organized in a manner that lends itself without difficulty to representation in PROLOG program form. In this respect their work was very similar to that of sixth form students at the same school three years earlier, as described in *Children program in PROLOG* (Ennals, 1981b), with the key difference that now we have six computers used by students instead of one used by the teacher.

9.4 SUBSEQUENT WORK

Since the last session at Ricards Lodge, we have been developing a Russian Revolution adventure game, arising from the work above, using the 'PLAN' front-end program to micro-PROLOG (Briggs, 1984).

As a narrative historian I must describe various aspects of the world of my chosen subject, in this case a revolutionary who is seeking to gain power. I can identify a number of places through which my central character will pass, each time typing

add place

and then giving the name, in this case: isolation, small group, party, parliament, government, control. Note that the places do not have to be physical or geographical, but can be conceptual, concerning parts of the structure of the problem domain.

I describe various objects as being found in different places, such as poverty in isolation, administrative support in the party.

I describe exits between different places in given directions, such as from small group to party towards power.

Fuller descriptions can be given, such as of a small group as "a group high on enthusiasm, low on practical ideas" and of Parliament as "an assembly of dubiously-elected members".

The initial location for my revolutionary is isolation. What follows is an example use of the story framework just described, the start of the revolutionary's quest for power. The story is started with the instruction 'go.', and then the individual participant indicates his chosen actions following the prompt '≫'.

go.

> You are standing in an area devoid of power and privilege
>
> You can exit: —
>> quick-route-to-power and
>> towards-power
> As you look around, you see: —
>> poverty and
>> revolutionary-ideas
> You are not carrying anything

≫   take revolutionary-ideas and move towards-power.

> You are standing in a group high on enthusiasm,
> low on practical ideas
>
> You can exit: —
>> towards-oblivion and
>> towards-power
> Near you, there is a-competent-organiser
> You have revolutionary-ideas

≫   create a-plan-of-action and take a-competent-organiser.

> You are standing in a group high on enthusiasm,
> low on practical ideas
>
> You can exit: —
>> towards-oblivion and
>> towards-power
> There is nothing of interest here
> You have:
>> revolutionary-ideas and
>> a-plan-of-action and
>> a-competent-organiser

≫   move towards-power.

A more complex version by Gareth Williams has undergone classroom trials, before forming part of his dissertation at Imperial College (Williams, 1984). Inga Watson's evaluation of the classroom use of the programs forms part of her dissertation at the Institute of Education (Watson, 1984).

9.5 CLASSROOM TRIALS OF THE 'REVOLT' PROGRAM

The simple version of 'Revolt' was demonstrated at Park House Middle School as an example use of 'PLAN'. Taking the idea of progressive description of an imaginary world in which one could explore with one's friends, different classes had developed adventures involving hidden treasure in a haunted house, and searching for the tomb of Tutankhamun. The classes took turns in either making a move in the 'game' or adding to the description, with the concept of what constituted 'winning' emerging gradually, together with routes to success, strategies and overall ideas of planning. Complex actions were defined in terms of component individual actions.

The same simple version was used with teachers at a workshop session at Southlands College, Roehampton Institute of Higher Education. Some explored applying the ideas of description and structure to different domains such as chemistry.

A prototype version of Gareth Williams 'Revolt' was used with two groups of fourth-year students at Garratt Green Comprehensive School. The first group had had the briefest of introductions to 'PLAN' the previous week, while the second group had built their own adventures, using actions provided in the 'PLAN' system.

In each case a demonstration of the program stimulated interest and discussion. Where possible, as at Southlands College, individual users were able to work on separate machines, while at Garratt Green there were two 8-station networks of Research Machines 480Zs available for use. Introductory documentation served to introduce individuals or small groups using the networks.

It is interesting to note the importance of particular subject knowledge in developing a specific serious example. Grasping the basic ideas of constructing the adventure-model is not difficult, but in order to describe new actions, new conditions for actions (for example you can start an insurrection if you have weapons, an army, and know-how) new descriptions and new synonyms subject knowledge is required, and skills of abstraction are called on.

The 'Revolt' program was put to its fullest test with a different sixth-form class at Ricards Lodge, with some past knowledge of twentieth century history and the Russian Revolution. They took an active part in developing and extending the program, replacing Gareth's tentative descriptions and slot-fillers with their own ideas. They described the party as "the workers democratic party", and took new actions such as "create propaganda" and "suppress aristocracy". They described internal dissent within the party, whereby the left wing and right wing both stuck to extreme points of view, while the moderates were prepared to compromise. They explored appropriate conditions for actions such as starting strikes and insurrections, reducing such major problems to sub-problems, which, if solved, would produce the required outcome.

The program proved easy to modify at the keyboard to incorporate the new changes and extensions, and it immediately incorporates the new level of detail in its subsequent operation. It was, however, increasingly slow-running on the Research Machines 380Z 56K machines.

There were clear areas where the students' ideas of the subject matter went beyond the capacity of the program to represent them. For example, it is open to the 'revolutionary' to support the workers, peasants, government, and other groups. Not unreasonably, the students wanted to know what the demands of these groups were, and to what extent an accommodation might be arrived at between people of conflicting views. Could a revolutionary sensibly support both the workers and the peasants? What consequences should flow from such a decision? To deal with such issues appropriately would require the modelling of belief systems in the manner of Colby and Abelson, whose ideology machine modelled the reasoning patterns of a "cold war warrior". This is beyond the scope of this program and the space available in today's classroom microcomputers.

10

Historical explanation using logic

This chapter draws heavily on the work of Robert Kowalski *Logic and belief* (1983) and Marek Sergot *A query-the-user facility for logic programming* (1983). The illustrative examples make use of Peter Hammond's 'CHIMP' program, a subset of his 'APES' Expert System Shell, and of Jonathan Briggs' 'PLAN' program which provides some facilities for describing simple adventures. I have developed the approach to historical explanation in previous papers. I should also acknowledge Alan Robinson's work 'Hume's two definitions of "cause"' (1968) and recent discussions with Robert Wolfson, particularly concerning the nuclear policy example.

10.1 INTRODUCTION

Historians are faced with an open world of events and phenomena with which they are concerned to come to terms, focusing on the area of human actions in the past. A first step is to describe some of the events and phenomena in a series of statements. A set of such statements must have a certain coherence if it is to be of use. It cannot aspire to completeness, nor can we sensibly talk of one-to-one correspondence between statements and the subject matter that they describe. Numerous statements could describe the same event.

We can regard the set of statements as a closed world. Answers to questions that are put to that set of statements will be restricted to the information that is contained in it. If we seek the explanation for an answer to a question it will be in terms of the individual statements and connections between them. Some of the statements will be straightforwardly factual and specific, others will be more general, involving existential and universal quantification over parts of this closed world, but not purporting to hold beyond the limits of stated knowledge.

The historian's set of statements can be represented as assertions and rules in the Horn clause form of predicate logic. I have earlier considered the construction and querying of historical databases with a variety of subject matter described in a common form: family genealogies, census information, soot collection records, bibliographic references, character descriptions, commodity prices, diaries, etc. The concern in this chapter is to explore problems of explanations of answers to questions in terms of the descriptions contained in the databases.

Let us borrow Kowalski's terminology, and regard databases additionally as belief systems. One advantage of this move is to introduce a common language for talking about answering questons overselves and answering questions to a database. Given a question ourselves, how can we set about answering it? This analysis owes a debt to the recent work applying logic to the British Nationality Act (Cory *et al.* 1984). We may be able to give an answer directly, from factual information that comes readily to mind. We may be able to infer an answer from a combination of rules and factual information that we have available. We might have to perform a calculation. We might have to ask for help, as information was required that was not immediately available. This help might be obtained by asking an expert, or possibly by asking for the question to be rephrased so that it might be answered.

Collingwood wrote (Collingwood, 1946), following Croce, of the dialogue of the historian with his evidence. The evidence is explicit, made up of facts and rules describing events and states of the world. The historian's belief system is implicit, drawn out in answer to questions raised by the evidence, and to issues of inconsistency. We can represent the two with a common language, and begin to investigate the area of collaborative problem solving involved in the task of historical explanation.

10.2 COLLABORATIVE PROBLEM SOLVING

Confession

The first examples make use of the interactive facilities of CHIMP (Hammond, 1984). In the CHIMP system, whenever there is no explicit information to help solve a problem, a question is posed to the user. We are concerned first of all with determining an individual's just deserts. In English we could say:

Someone deserves damnation if he has committed a deadly sin of which he does not repent.

Someone deserves commendation if he has committed something useful that does not only benefit himself.

Our database contains two rules:

x deserves damnation if   x committed y and
                          y is-a deadly-sin and
                          not x repents y

x deserves commendation if   x committed y and
                              y useful and
                              not y only-benefits x

It contains no specific factual information: that will have to be gleaned from the user. I wish to find out my fate.

> which (x: Richard deserves x)

and the system replies with a series of questions, to which I can respond.

> which (x: Richard committed x)?
>> answer is secret-drinking
>> answer is overtime
>> answer is end
> is (secret-drinking is-a deadly-sin)? (yes/no) yes
> is (Richard repents secret-drinking)? (yes/no) no
> ===〉damnation
> is (overtime is-a deadly-sin)? (yes/no) no
> is (secret-drinking useful ( )? (yes/no) no
> is (overtime useful)? (yes/no) yes
> is (overtime only-benefits Richard)? (yes/no) no
> ===〉commendation
> no (more) answers

As well as having answered our original question, some information has been transferred from the user to the system, embodying the answers to each of the questions. If we regard the user and the system as jointly concerned in a problem-solving activity, we can say that no new knowledge has been added overall, but some implicit knowledge on the part of the user has been made explicit.

Inquisition

A related historical example concerned the process of Inquisition. We can describe what it is to be a fully conformist member of the Catholic Church, accepting all the beliefs of the Pope.

> x conformist if (forall y is-a Pope and
>   y believes z
>   then x accepts z)

We know that

> John-Paul is-a Pope

and his beliefs are well-known

> John-Paul believes (abortion is wrong)
> John-Paul believes (priests should be celibate)
> John-Paul believes (church and state should get on together)

What is less clear is what the individual under Inquisition believes. The fate of heretics can be unpleasant.

> x heretic if not x conformist

The views of the prisoner Tom should emerge under interrogation, so we ask

is (Tom heretic)

and the system responds

is (Tom accepts (abortion is wrong))? (yes/no) yes
is (Tom accepts (priests should be celibate))? (yes/no) no

with the verdict

Yes, Tom heretic

For our records we can check that his responses have been recorded:

list accepts
You confirmed the following
Tom accepts (abortion is wrong)

Nuclear Arms Talks

The third, more complex, example concerns arms policies by the USA and USSR. At the simplest level we can describe three different outcomes of a round of decision making, with an arms race, peace talks, or a lead for one side:

arms-race outcome if USA decides arm and
                      USSR decides arm

peace-talks outcome if USA decides stop and
                       USSR decides stop

(x lead) outcome if x decides arm and
                    y decides stop

What, then, is the outcome? It is up to the users:

which (x:x outcome)
which (x:x decides arm)?
        answer is USSR
        answer is end
which (x:x decides stop)?
        answer is USA
        answer is end
        ===⟩ (USSR lead)
No (more) answers

We now broaden the example to allow for three alternative decisions by each side: arms freezes, or disarms. We also seek information as to the relative strengths of the two sides before each side has to make its policy choice.

x chooses-policy if   y ON (arms freezes disarms) and
                       x rival-of z and
                       x relative-position (x to z) and
                       x choice y

We describe the case of the two superpowers:

> USA rival-of USSR
> USSR rival-of USA

Relative position is defined in terms of the number of arms held on each side:

> x relative-position (ahead to y) if x number-of-arms z and
> y number-of-arms X and
> X LESS z

> x relative-position (parity to y) if x number-of-arms z and
> y number-of-arms z and
> not x EQ y

> x relative-position (behind to y) if x number-of-arms z and
> y number-of-arms X and
> z LESS X

Number-of-arms is here arbitrarily defined as the total number of planes, ships, and missiles.

> x number-of-arms y if x total-planes z and
> x total-ships X and
> x total-missiles Y and
> (z X Y) sums-to y

Let us now find out about USA policy, by asking:

> which (x: USA chooses-policy x)

We need in turn to answer questions from the system

> which (x: USA total-planes x)?
> answer is 500
> answer is end
> which (x: USA total-ships x)?
> answer is 400
> answer is end
> which (x: USA total-missiles x)?
> answer is 1500
> answer is end
> which (x: USSR total-planes x)?
> answer is 700
> answer is end
> which (x: USSR total-ships x)?
> answer is 300
> answer is end
> which (x: USSR total-missiles x)?
> answer is 1600
> answer is end

is (USA choice arms)? (yes/no) no
is (USA choice freezes)? (yes/no) yes
　　　===⟩ freezes
is (USA choice disarms)? (yes/no) no
　　　No (more) answers

It is much quicker to establish USSR policy:

which (x: USSR chooses-policy x)

As information has already been gathered on relative strengths, we can proceed directly to:

is (USSR choice arms)? (yes/no) no
is (USSR choice freezes)? (yes/no) yes
　　　===⟩ freezes
is (USSR disarms)? (yes/no) no
　　　No (more) answers

We might want to describe the different states of affairs that obtain depending on the policies chosen by both sides, for example

stable conjunction if　x chooses-policy freezes and
　　　　　　　　　　　　y chooses-policy freezes and
　　　　　　　　　　　　not x EQ y

In this case we can check whether there is a stable conjunction:

is (stable conjunction)
Yes, stable conjunction

We can now check up on the relative strengths of the two sides:

which (x y:x relative-position y)
　　　===⟩ USSR (ahead to USA)
　　　===⟩ USA (behind to USSR)
　　　No (more) answers

So far we have made no specific use of this information in decision making and we might want to add further rules clarifying policy choices as observed, for example:

x choice arms if x relative-position (behind to y) and
　　　　　　　　x rival-of y

At this stage an important distinction must be drawn between explanation and prediction. Some social scientists are concerned with predicting future behaviour in terms of observed norms and regularities established in the past. Historians are concerned with a coherent explanation of the past in terms of their own collection of statements. There is a sense in which historians may predict the past by establishing the likelihood of a particular statement prior to receiving further confirmation. Explanations need to hold over the domain of the belief system, and must be capable of modification in the light of new information which may be added to the belief system. Rules in this context have descriptive and explanatory force. They are not necessarily concerned with physical causation, and may more often be taken up with reasons for action. Explanation is often a matter of redescription, but also concerns plans and intentions (Harre 1974, Von Wright, 1971).

10.3 NARRATIVE AND DESCRIPTION

History is not concerned merely with static states of affairs, but with change over time. We must be aware of the temporal component, explicit or implicit, in any historical statement. As historians, we are not concerned with specifying and building complex temporal systems for future use, but with describing and explaining complex problems that develop over time. Often a partial account can provide illumination for the whole.

Earlier I described *ad hoc* approaches to time-handling problems in role-play based computer-aided historical simulations. Most descriptions of unchanging information that would hold true throughout the simulation activity lacked a temporal component. Key chronological historical events were described according to their year of occurrence or period of efficacy. Within the simulation activity there were a series of decision-making periods (12 in the case of the Russian Revolution simulation). Decisions were described with the round number. Certain generalizations held true according to the round number. Certain documentary references were to be consulted during particular rounds, and general advice was available from the directing program depending on the round.

In current work, Jonathan Briggs has developed a simple 'TIME' supervisor that in effect gives a formal framework to the handling of decision-making rounds outlined above. Under this supervisor decisions or statements are time-stamped, and selected consequences are made explicit at the end of each round. We could, for example, have a rule that someone becomes Prime Minister if the Queen chooses that person. Our supervisor can be told that 'becomes' 'could-happen':

> x becomes Prime-Minister if Queen chooses x
> becomes could-happen

We now start the 'clock', and add information about the royal . . .

> user 1
> 1 》 add (Queen chooses Margaret)

Our decisions over, we type

> end

and the system tells us

> Margaret becomes Prime-Minister

> 2》

It has now moved us on to the next 'round'.

Typically, historical information does not arrive ready time-stamped, and historical explanation has little to do with dates. Temporal ordering is crucial, and a series of disparate events can be better understood in sequence. Often the way in which an historian sets about explaining a given statement is by telling a story. The story does not purport to be the whole truth and nothing but the truth, but it sets out to shed light. Description is crucial to the historian's story: it must be accurate but above all coherent. Characters, places, groups, social customs, laws, and traditions — all are amenable to description using facts and rules.

In the previous chapter we considered the use of the 'PLAN' program to aid in story-telling and 'adventure game' styles of simulation, with particular emphasis on the example of the revolutionary.

The purpose of such a program is to give some coherence to a complex subject, to motivate thought and discussion over extensions to the description, further actions that the agent should be able to perform, and reasons for taking different decisions. An obviously desirable extension would be the involvement of several agents, whose actions can affect the environment and each other. Another would be the access to text from disk to provide detailed evidence for the user to encounter on his travels and interrogate. If we take the classic murder mystery example, we can envisage our detective encountering databases of information in the library, or consulting a medical expert system to help him in determining the cuase of death of the unfortunate victim. We are concerned with history as adventure as well as of adventures.

10.4 CONCLUSION

I have not here given examples of the explanation facilities provided by APES which are documented elsewhere (Sergot, 1983, Hammond, 1983, Cory *et al.* 1984). They have not been available for machines used in schools, though this will change with the falling cost of microcomputers.

The view developed here has been a particular view of historical explanation, and it has been argued that logic and logic programming offer appropriate tools for understanding concepts of explanation, for modelling the interaction of the historian and his evidence, for developing narrative descriptive accounts, and for assisting in explanation of historical conclusions in terms of historical statements.

11

Case study programs

11.1 THE MARSEILLES CONNECTION

The restaurant example

Marseilles has a deserved reputation for the quality of its restraurants. Perhaps in order to spread good eating habits together with PROLOG, Henry Kanoui chose to introduce PROLOG II to non-specialist users with a motivating example derived from a restaurant menu. We have used the same example with teachers in London (where there is considerable respect for French food) and introduce it here using micro-PROLOG, and with an adapation of Kanoui's explanatory text.

To show how things are done in PROLOG, we have constructed an elementary example which describes the menu of a restaurant. The objects which interest us are the menu items which can be eaten, and an initial set of relations which classify the menu items into hors d'oeuvres, a main dish of meat or fish, and desserts. This menu constitutes a small database which can be written as follows:

Artichauts-Melanie	hors-d-oeuvre
Truffes-sous-le-sel	hors-d-oeuvre
Cresson-oeuf-poche	hors-d-oeuvre
Bar-aux-algues	fish
Chapon-farci	fish
Grillade-de-boeuf	meat
Poulet-au-tilleul	meat
Sorbet-aux-poires	dessert
Fraises-chantilly	dessert
Melon-en-surprise	dessert

The relations which we have defined introduce both the objects (the menu items) and their classification. For example

Cresson-oeuf-poche   hors-d-oeuvre

indicates that the Cresson-oeuf-poche is an hors d'oeuvre and nothing more.

When we have a database, we can ask questions about it. A question of the form: "Is Cresson-oeuf-poche an hors d'oeuvre?" is translated by

&. is (Cresson-oeuf-poche hors-d-oeuvre)

A search is then made to see if this information is known: the answer is YES. On the other hand

&. is (Salade-de-tomates hors-d-oeuvre)

receives a negative response, because the database does not contain such information. Suppose now that we want to know what hors d'oeuvre we can eat. It would be tedious to ask the sequence of questions

&. is (Salade-de-tomates hors-d-oeuvre)
&. is (Artichauts-Melanie hors-d-oeuvre) etc

and to wait each time for a YES or NO response. We really want to ask:

What are the hors d'oeuvres?

or better: what are the objects 'x' which are the hors d'oeuvres?
without needing to know what objects 'x' represents. Here the name 'x' does not denote any one particular object but all the objects in the set (possibly empty) of those which possess the property of being an hors d'oeuvre. Such an 'x' is called a 'variable'. In our case the question is translated as

&. which (x:x hors-d-oeuvre)

and PROLOG responds

Artichauts-Melanie
Truffes-sous-le-sel
Cresson-oeuf-poche
No (more) answers

Using the initial relations in the database, we can construct more general or complex relations. For example, using the relations 'meat' and 'fish' which express the fact that the argument is a basic dish of meat or fish, we can define the relation 'main-dish' which says that a 'main-dish' is either meat or fish; we write this

x main-dish if x meat
x main-dish if x fish

and read it: x is a main dish if x is meat
                 x is a main dish if x is fish

Here the variable 'x' is used in each of the two rules to designate respectively all the meat dishes and all the fish dishes.

Note that the scope of a variable is restricted to the rule in which it is defined, and thus the variable 'x' in the first rule is not tied in any way to the variable 'x' in the second rule.

In our example, the question "What are the main dishes?" is translated as

&. which (x:x main-dish)

and produces the responses:

Grillade-de-boeuf
Poulet-au-tilleul
Bar-aux-Algues
Chapon-farci
No (more) answers

Now let us compose a meal; following the usual rules, a meal consists of an hors d'oeuvre, a main dish (meat or fish), and a dessert. A meal is thus a triplet 'x y z' where 'x' is an hors d'oeuvre, 'y' a main-dish, and 'z' a dessert. This is expressed very naturally by the rule:

meal (x y z) if   x hors-d-oeuvre and
                  y main-dish and
                  z dessert

which is read:

'x y z' satisfies the relation 'meal' if 'x' satisfies the relation 'hors-d-oeuvre', and if 'y' satisfies the relation 'main-dish' and if 'z' satisfies the relation 'dessert'.

More generally, we have defined a new relation as a conjunction of three other relations.

To the question, "what are the meals?" that is to say:

&. which (x y z: meal (x y z))

PROLOG responds

Artichauts-Melanie Grillade-de-boeuf Sorbet-aux-poires
Artichauts-Melanie Grillade-de-boeuf Fraises-chantilly
   . . .
   . . .
   . . .
   . . .
   . . .
   . . .

a list of the 36 possible combinations.

Keeping the same set of relations, we ask a somewhat more complex question: "Which meals have fish as the main dish?" This is translated by

which (x y z: meal (x y z) and
    y fish)

which expresses the conjunction of the two conditions which we want to see satisfied. The program will print out the 18 possible solutions.

Next we introduce a small refinement into our database of meals by introducing the calorie count of each menu item proposed:

Artichauts-Melanie	calories	150
Cresson-oeuf-poche	calories	202
Truffes-sous-le-sel	calories	212
Grillade-de-boeuf	calories	532
Poulet-au-tilleul	calories	400
Bar-aux-algues	calories	292
Chapon-farci	calories	254
Sorbet-aux-poires	calories	223
Fraises-chantilly	calories	289
Melon-en-surprise	calories	122

The sentence:

Chapon-farci calories 254

is interpreted as "the portion of Chapon-farci served contains 254 calories".

If we want to know the calorie counts of each hors d'oeuvre, we ask:

&. which (x y:x hors-d-oeuvre and
     x calories y)

Artichauts-Melanie 150
Truffes-sous-le-sel 202
Cresson-oeuf-poche 202
No (more) answers

A more curious gourmet might want to know the total calorie count of all of the constituents of a meal. To achieve this, we defined the following relation:

value (x y z X) if x calories Y and
     y calories Z and
     z calories x1 and
     (Y Z x1) sums-to X

where X is the sum of the calorie counts of each of the constituents of the meal. To learn these values, ask the question:

&. which (x y z X: meal (x y z) and
                     value (x y z X))

which yields

Artichauts-Melanie Grillade-de-boeuf Sorvet-aux-poires 905
Artichauts-Melanie Grillade-de-boeuf Fraises-Chantilly 971 etc

We are naturally led to define a slimming meal by:

slimming-meal (x y z) if meal (x y z) and
                         value (x y z X) and
                         X LESS 800

which defines a slimming-meal as one with less than 800 calories. The question:

&. which (x y: slimming-meal (x y z))

gives the list of answers:

Artichauts-Melanie Poulet-au-tilleul Sorbet-aux-poires etc

We finish with this example by asking:

&. which (x y z: slimming-meal (x y z) and
                    y meat)

"which slimming-meals have meat as a main-dish?"
The results are

Artichauts-Melanie Poulet-au-tilleul Sorbet-aux-poires
Artichauts-Melanie Poulet-au-tilleul Melon-en-surprise
Truffes-sous-le-sel Poulet-au-tilleul Melon-en-surprise
Cresson-oeuf-poche Poulet-au-tilleul Melon-en-surprise
No (more) answers

Food, Folksong and Interior Decor

Anthropologists such as Levi-Strauss have given considerable emphasis to food and meals in their studies of different societies. We have tried to use PROLOG as a tool to help us to describe and make sense of our world. One of our first examples working with teachers in Marseilles using micro-PROLOG concerned a well-known Provencale folk song. Once we had described the days of the week and the names of items to be purchased from the market, together with a rule to determine pairs of rhyming words, a program generated the song according to the structure that we had described (a structure somwhat similar to the English song 'One man went to mow').

The city of Marseilles dates from Greek times, and has always contained a variety of communities in the different 'quarters'. In the late seventeenth century, for a variety of reasons including the city's tradition of freethinking independence and even rebellion, King Louis XIV ordered a vast programme to extend the city directed by his local officials, including the demolition of some of the fortifications and the construction of attrative houses in the suburbs for the gentry and senior royal officials. Social historians have been trying to establish what effect this had on the life of the people in the different quartiers. Beatrice Henin, some of whose work was translated earlier, has been studying leasehold documents drawn up by notaries and inventories of properties taken at the time of death, making use of a computer in her analysis of the mass of complex data. Towards the end of her research she has become interested in the interior decor of houses of people from the different social classes, and has been using PROLOG to help in the analysis of different pictures, largely with religious themes, recorded as being on the walls of various rooms. She has reached some fascinating conclusions, developing a model which may be usefully applied, for instance, to Protestant and Catholic families in England in the seventeenth century. This is consistent with the modelling tradition in urban history and sociology, whereby research experience derived from the study of a city such as Chicago, London, Paris, or Boston can then be applied to further cases such as Marseilles, with the objective of understanding and making sense of complex phenomena.

11.2 AN ELECTION PROGRAM

We start by representing the results of an election as a program in micro-PROLOG, as follows:

Smith	votes	500
Brown	votes	1275
White	votes	382
Green	votes	4380
Bloggs	votes	45

We can also mention the party affiliation of each candidate:

Smith	party	Liberal
Brown	party	Conservative
White	party	National-Front
Green	party	Labour
Bloggs	party	Communist

One candidate beats another if he receives more votes. This can be expressed as a rule:

    x beats y if   x votes z and
                   y votes X and
                   X LESS z

The candidate elected is the one whose total of votes is not beaten by any other candidate:

    x elected if   x votes y and
                   not z beats x

Questions can be asked such as:

(1) Was Brown the Conservative Party candidate?
    is (Brown party Conservative)
(2) How many votes did Smith receive?
    which (x: Smith votes x)
(3) Which candidates stood for which parties?
    which (x y: x party y)
(4) How many votes did the Communist party candidate receive?
    which (x: y party Communist and
            y votes x)
(5) Which candidates beat White?
    which (x: x beat White)
(6) Was the Conservative Party candidate elected?
    is (x party Conservative and x elected)
(7) Who was elected?
    which (x: x elected)
(8) Under current British electoral law candidates forfeit their deposits if they
    fail to receive one in eight of the votes cast (12.5%). It will be useful to
    know what percentage of the total vote has been achieved by each candidate.

    x percent-vote y if x votes z and
                        X total-vote and
                        TIMES (Y X z) and
                        TIMES (Y 100 y)

    x loses deposit if   x percent-vote y and
                         y LESS 12.5

    x total-vote if y isall (z: X votes z) and
                        y sums-to x

    (x) sums-to x
    (x|y) sums-to z if y sums-to X and
                        SUM (X x z)

(9) Which candidates lost their deposits?
    which (x: x loses deposit)
(10) What percentage of the vote was achieved by each candidate?
    which (x y: x percent-vote y)

We should add some information about the political parties involved in the
election, and their relative postions on the political spectrum:

Communist	left-of	Labour
Labour	left-of	Liberal
Liberal	left-of	Conservative
Conservative	left-of	National-Front

    x to-left-of y if x left-of y

x to-left-of y if x left-of z and
    z left-of y
x to-right-of y if y to-left-of x

(11) Which parties are to the left of the National-Front?
  which (x: x to-left-of National Front)
(12) Is the Liberal Party to the right of the Conservative Party?
  is (Liberal to-right-of Conservative)

All EEC countries apart from Britain used proportional representation in the 1984 European Elections. Here the votes of the parties are significant as well as the votes of individual candidates. In this example we take the results in the one election and see what the consequences would be if all 650 British parliamentary seats were allocated on the basis of party votes instead of the 'first past the post system'.

x party-percent y if z party x and
        z percent-vote y
x proportional-seats y if x party-percent z and
          X total-seats and
          TIMES (X z Y) and
          TIMES (y 100 Y)
 650 total-seats

(13) What percentage of the votes was gained by each party?
  which (x y: x party-percent y)
(14) How many seats overall are awarded to each party?
  which (x y: x proportional-seats y)

Classes taught by the author at Sweyne School, Rayleigh, in Essex, held a mock general election in 1979. Student candidates for five political parties prepared manifestos and addressed election meetings. On general election day the whole school voted, a total of 896 votes. The results were compared with the mock general election at the school in the autumn of 1974, and the 'swing' in votes was calculated. A table had been drawn up of marginal constituencies around the United Kingdom, and the swing in percentage of votes that would be required for the seat to change hands. The Conservative candidate, Mary Jones, won the school election, and a substantial Conservative majority was predicted for Margaret Thatcher nationally. Below are some excerpts from the report of the election in Datalink, for 10 May 1979.

"It's a Tory victory, and the majority is a spanking great 324! If that doesn't tie in with the election results which have been monopolizing the whole of the media for the last fortnight, that's because it's a different election altogether.
This microcosm of the real world was enacted at a school in Rayleigh, Essex, on the same day as the more well-known General Election, and was plotted (as in the real world) by computer."

On election day itself the *Daily Telegraph* reported:

> "Pupils at Sweyne School, a comprehensive at Rayleigh, Essex, will be using a computer to forecast the election result. It has been programmed to predict the national result based on the voting patterns of two elections staged at the school."

The educational purpose of the activity was to give the students insight into what happens in elections: how campaigns can be run, how political arguments can be expressed, how votes are counted, and the significance of concepts of 'majority' and 'swing', hard to describe in the abstract. In this case there was the added bonus of forming part of the news ourselves, and seeing the difference between what was reported and what actually happened.

The election simulation activity continued the following year, when Sweyne School was called in to help the local *Southend Evening Echo* in predicting the results of the Southend East by-election. This is how the *Evening Echo* described the results of an eve-of-poll survey, in their issue of Wednesday 12 March 1980:

> "Teddy Taylor will scrape back to Parliament in tomorrow's Southend East by-election, according to an *Echo* poll.
>
> Mr Taylor will hold the seat for the Conservatives by a mere 390 votes, it is predicted.
>
> But his share of the poll could rise dramatically if there's a low poll. . . .
>
> The *Echo* survey was based on advice from one of Britain's leading opinion poll firms.
>
> And its results were analysed by Rayleigh Sweyne School's computer, the 'Sweynometer.'
>
> The computer, highly successful in past elections, was fed with a host of information, including the fact that the lower the poll, the bigger the Tory advantage was likely to be."

To further compound this growing mythology of the power of the educational use of computers in studying elections, here is the report of the *Times Educational Supplement* of 28 March 1980:

> "Fears of a Teddy Taylor defeat in the recent Southend by-election had all the magicians and astrologers in the Conservative Central Office invoking their most special spells. But all they needed to do was consult the work of the local paper, the *Evening Echo,* and the pupils of the general election — with remarkable accuracy.
>
> Last year fifth-form history pupils at the school worked out a computer programme on their Research Machines 380Z (known as the 'Sweynometer') to predict the outcome of the general election — with remarkable accuracy.
>
> In the recent by-election the local paper did its own survey of voters and called in the school to process the findings. The day before voting the

Echo/Sweyne poll forecast a majority for Mr Taylor of 'a mere 390 votes'. The actual result — a majority of 430 votes.''

By the time the story reached the pages of the Department of Industry magazine *View* in the summer of 1980, the election result had clearly been predicatable once one knew the source of the eve-of-poll predictions!

"Few people in Southend were surprised when Teddy Taylor scraped home in the March by-election by a majority of 430 votes. The *Southend Evening Echo* had predicted a 390 majority. What many readers did not not was that this prediction had come from the Sweyne School in Rayleigh, Essex. The school is in the forefront of classroom computer technology and used their 'Sweynometer' to calculate the result. . . their reputation for accurate psephology is the result of mock general elections conducted by the school."

The students who were involved in both election programs, and who served as 'consultants' in the history lessons of younger classes, developing programs to help difficult aspects of simulations, learnt one particular lesson from their encounters with the real world of elections and press coverage: do not believe everything you read in the papers. For all of the students who participated even just by casting a vote, it provided a valuable insight into different kinds of evidence and their reliability. They had been present, and most of the journalists came by their information at least second-hand.

And the role of the computer in all this? To act as a catalyst, to help provide a valuable educational experience, to open up new areas of interest. Serious psephology is a job for serious psephologists, and cannot be attempted with a 32K microcomputer. Computing, however, is too important to be left to computer scientists.

11.3 SAXON PLACE-NAMES PROGRAM

This program was developed at Bishop Wand School, Sunbury, based on a worksheet prepared by Mrs Elizabeth Hossain, and using micro-PROLOG on the Sinclair Spectrum. It is concerned first of all with identifying towns as being a likely Saxon origin by virtue of the ending of the place-name, which also gives an indication of the original meaning of the name. There then follows a more detailed study of place-names in the Sunbury area, with the earliest known spellings, earliest dates known, and probable meanings. The information is then available for interrogation in a number of ways. Details can be changed in the light of further research, or details of further towns can be added. First, we identify towns of Saxon origin:

x origin Saxon if x ending y and
           y ON (ton ham ley ford burgh cot stead ing hurst)

x ending y if z STRINGOF x and
        APPEND (x y z) and
        Y STRINGOF y

(the relations ON, STRINGOF, and APPEND are built-into Spectrum micro-PROLOG using SIMPLE)

Then, we record the likely meanings of the endings:

ton	means	farm
ham	means	(farm or village)
ley	means	(clearing in the forest)
ford	means	(shallow crossing in the river)
burgh	means	stronghold
bury	means	stronghold
cot	means	(solitary cottage)
stead	means	(house or farm)
ing	means	(family settlement)
hurst	means	woodland

Questions:

(1) Is Sandhurst of Saxon orgin?
    is (Sandhurst origin Saxon)

    x meaning-involves y if x ending z and
                    z ON (ton ham ley ford burgh bury cot stead
                            ing hurst) and
                    z means y

(2) What does Sandhurst's meaning involve?
    which (x: Sandhurst meaning-involves x)

We then add the more detailed database of information about towns in the Sunbury area, with rules to help us pick out particular items.

Ashford	details	(Ecelesford 969 (ecle's ford))
Chertsey	details	(Cerotaesi 730 (Cero's Island))
Feltham	details	(Fyletham 882 (hay farm))
Fulwell	details	(Fulewella 1086 (foul well))
Halliford	details	((Halyon Forde) 962 (holy ford))
Hampton	details	(Hamntone 1086 (settlement by meadows))
Hansworth	details	(Handeword 1086 (high enclosure))
Hounslow	details	(Hundeslouwe 1242)
Kempton	details	(Chenetone 1086 (Chen's farm))
Kingston	details	(Cyningeston 838 (King's farm))
Laleham	details	(Lealham 1986 (water meadows))
Littleton	details	(Litleton 1185 (a small farm))
Shepperton	details	(Scepertun 959 (Somebody's farm))
Staines	details	(Stana 969 (milestones))
Sunbury	details	(Sunnabyrg 960 (Sunna's stronghold))
Teddington	details	(Tudintun 969 (Tudda's farm))
Twickenham	details	(Twiccanham 704 (Twicca's farm village))
Walton	details	(Waleton 1086 (town of the Britons))

The rules use patterns to pick out elements of the lists following the name of relation 'details':

x earliest-spelling y if x details (y|z)
x first-known y if x details (z y|X)
x probable-meaning y if x details (z Y y)

(3) What was the earliest spelling of Kingston?
which (x: Kingston earliest-spelling x)

(4) Was Hamntone the earliest spelling of Hampton?
is (Hampton earliest-spelling Hamntone)

(5) When was Sunbury first known?
which (x: Sunbury first-known x)

(6) Which places were first known in 1086?
which (x: x first-known 1086)

(7) What was the probable meaning of Twickenham?
which (x: Twickenham probable-meaning x)

(8) What were the first known dates of each of the places?
which (x y: x first-known y)

(9) What were the probable meanings of the places that were first known in 1086?

which (x y: x first-known 1086 and
              x probable-meaning y)

x older-than y if x first-known z and
                  y first-known X and
                  z LESS X

x oldest if x first-known y and
            not z older-than x

(10) Which places are older than Hampton?
which (x: x older-than Hampton)

(11) Is Twickenham the oldest place in the area?
is (Twickenham oldest)

We may want to determine in what century each town was first known:

x century y if TIMES (z 100 x) and
               z INT X and
               SUM (X 1 y)

(the relations TIMES, INT, SUM and LESS are built into Spectrum micro-PROLOG using SIMPLE)

(12) In what century was Halliford first known?
which (x: Halliford first-known y and
          y century x)

(13) In what century was the oldest town first known?
which (x: y oldest and
          y first-known z and
          z century x)

(14) What details are available for Ashford?
which (x: Ashford details x)

11.4 BIBLIOGRAPHIC PROGRAM

We may wish to make reference to books and papers that we have read concerning our particular interests. Conventional filing systems offer us restricted access to the information that we may need to help us with a variety of problems.

The subject chosen here is that of History and Computing, a growing field.

For books, we want information on
author title publisher date keywords

e.g. book ((Collingwood R G) (The Idea of History) (Oxford) 1946 (Philosophy
                                                                    History))
book ((White A R (ed)) (The Philosophy of Action) (OUP) 1968 (Philosophy))
book ((Glover J (ed)) (The Philosophy of Mind) (OUP) 1976 (Philosophy)
book ((Dickinson A, Lee P J (eds)) (History Teaching and Historical
            Understanding) (Heinemann) 1977 (History Education))
book ((Ennals J R) (Beginning micro-PROLOG) (Ellis Horwood and
            Heinemann) 1982 (Education Computing Logic History))

For papers, we want information on:
author title source date keywords

e.g. paper ((Davidson D) (Actions, Reasons and Causes) (White A R ed) 1968
            (Philosophy History))
paper ((Ennals J R) (Simulations and Computers) (Teaching History June)
            1980 (History Education Computing))

Information is accessible from both sources through the use of rules:

x author-of y if book (x y|z)
x author-of y if paper (x y|z)
(x y) reference (z X) if book (x z X y Y)
(x y) reference (z X) if paper (x z X y Y)
(x y) reference (z X) if paper (x z Z y Y) and
                        (Z y) reference (z X)
x keyword-in (y z) if book (y X Y z Z) and
                x ON Z
x keyword-in (y z) if paper (y X Y z Z) and
                x ON Z

Some example questions:
(1) What has Davidson D published?
which (x: (Davidson D) author-of x)
(2) What is the full reference for Collingwood R G (1946)?
which (x: ((Collingwood R G) 1946) reference x)

(3) What are references for publications concerning History?
which (x y: History keyword-in x and x reference y)

x publisher-of (y z X) if (y X) reference (z x)
x year-of (y z X) if (y x) reference (z X)

(4) What has been published since 1975?
which (x: y year-of x and
1975 LESS y)

(5) What have OUP published?
which (x: (OUP) publisher-of x)

(6) Were any publications concerning Computing produced before 1982?
is (Computing keyword-in (x y) and
y LESS 1982)

11.5 THE ENGLAND CRICKET TEAM

The England cricket team to play Pakistan has been announced, together with the age and number of tests played by each team member. We can represent this information as a program:

(Willis R G D (capt))	has	(34 86)
(Smith C L)	has	(25 4)
(Gatting M W)	has	(26 26)
(Gower D I)	has	(25 26)
(Lamb A J)	has	(29 18)
(Randall D W)	has	(33 43)
(Botham I T)	has	(28 66)
(Marks V J)	has	(28 3)
(Taylor R W)	has	(42 54)
(Cook N G B)	has	(27 3)
(Cowans N G)	has	(22 10)

x age y if x has (y z)
x played y if x has (z y)

Some example questions:
(1) How old is I T Botham?
which (x: (Botham I T) age x)

(2) Which players are aged less than 30?
which (x: x age y and
y LESS 30)

(3) How many tests has Willis played?
which (x: (Willis|y) played x)

(4) Who has played more tests than M W Gatting?
which (x: (Gatting M W) played y and
x played z and
y LESS z)

We can define some new relations to ease the process of querying:

> x older-than y if x age z and
> > y age X and
> > X LESS z

> x more-test-than y if x played z and
> > y played X and
> > X LESS z

> x average-age if y isall (z: X age z) and
> > y average x

> x average-tests if   y isall (z: X played z) and
> > y average x

> x average y if x sums-to z and
> > x length X and
> > TIMES (y X z)

> (x) sums-to x
> (x|y) sums-to z if y sums-to X and
> > SUM (X x z)
> ( ) length 0
> (x|y) length z if y length X and
> > SUM (X 1 z)

(5) What is the average age of the England team?
which (x: x average-age)
(6) Have the team on average played more than 20 tests?
is (x average-tests and
    20 LESS x)
(7) Who has a less than average age but has played more than the average
number of test matches?

> which (x: x age y and
> > z average-age and
> > y LESS z and
> > x played X and
> > Y average-tests and
> > Y LESS X)

11.6 SOCIAL CLASS PROGRAM

Sociologists are inclined to divide society into a number of smaller classes. There are several variations on this theme; when the Registrar-General takes a census in which the government tries to collect basic information on the population of Great Britain, he uses a method known as the Registrar-General's classification. Other organizations and sociologists may use slightly different methods, but they are all alike in that they all group people according to their occupation:

x class 1 if x occupation Professional
x class 2 if x occupation Intermediate
x class 3 if x occupation Skilled-manual
x class 4 if x occupation Semi-skilled-manual
x class 5 if x occupation Unskilled-manual

This classification can be applied to existing census data, or when carrying out a survey. It depends on an agreed classification of jobs into occupational groups. Answers on classification can be arrived at either by consulting an explicit database of facts and rules, by asking an expert, or by asking the user of the classification system.

If we take the last, most general, case, we can add further rules in micro-PROLOG to enable the system to query the user to help it solve problems of social class identification. We also load the 'TOLD' module (which is provided on the cassette or disk with micro-PROLOG):

x occupation y if x job z and z classed-as y
x classed-as y if (x classed-as y) is-told

With the addition of the two rules above, problems of social class identification will be solved, but the knowledge about the occupational grouping of particular jobs will be lost.

This deficiency can be overcome by adding sentences about the grouping of a job to the program, and consulting such sentences before querying the user. This involves rewriting the 'classed-as' program as follows:

x classed-as y if x grouping y and
   /
x classed-as y if (x classed-as y) is-told and
    (x grouping y) add

As at the beginning of the development of this classification system there will be no sentences about 'grouping', we must add:

grouping data-rel

Note that this program can be used together with census programs in micro-PROLOG to extend the descriptive and explanatory power of the student or researcher. The user is asked to participate in the amalgamation of two social scientific models, and his answers to questions are incorporated into the resulting new model.

In the cases where the program does not already contain information about jobs, two rules similar to those above can be added:

x job y if x has-job y and
   /
x job y if (x job y) is-told and
    (x has-job y) add
has-job data-rel

The rules for occupational classification of social class remain the same, though in different situations, for pragmatic reasons, they may be applied to information about occupations and jobs in different ways.

11.7 WEATHER FORECAST PROGRAM

Each day many newspapers print a weather report, gathered from correspondents in different towns around the world. In each case, a record was taken of the type of weather, and the temperature in Centigrade and Fahrenheit. For example, the record:

record (Ajaccio R 12 54)

together with the rules:

x weather rain if record (x R y z)
x temp-C y if record (x z y X)
x temp-F y if record (x z X y)

enable us to have access to a range of information about Ajaccio, using simple questions:

Is the weather in Ajaccio rainy?
is (Ajaccio weather rain)
YES

What is the temperature in Ajaccio, in Centigrade?
which (x: Ajaccio temp-C x)
12
No (more) answers

In our program, records have been kept of 95 towns. Similar questions to the above can be asked of the whole database:

Which places are sunny?
which (x: x weather sunny)
Athens
Bermuda
Bristol
(33 answers in all)

We can narrow down our search for the sun:

Which places are sunny and have a temperature of over 25 Centigrade?
which (x: x weather sunny and x temp-C y and 25 LESS y)
Cairo
Cape Town
Karachi
New-Delhi
Perth
Riyadh

Tel-Aviv
No (more) answers

We can check the position at home:

What was the weather and Fahrenheit temperature in London?
which (x y: London weather x and London Temp-F y)
cloudy 45
No (more) answers

We can make comparisons:

What places had the same temperature as London, and what was their weather like?
which (x y: x same-temp-as London and x weather y)
Dublin rain
Edinburgh sunny
London cloudy
Munich fair
Prague fair
Stockholm sunny
No (more) answers

What was the average temperature in Fahrenheit?
which (x: x ave-temp-F)
58.073684
No (more) answers

The programs for "same-temp-as" and "ave-temp-F" take forms that will be familiar by now:

x same-temp-as y if x temp-F z and
                        y temp-F z
x ave-temp-F if   y isall (z : X temp-F z) and
                        y average x

11.8 SOIL IDENTIFICATION PROGRAM (USING CHIMP)

A common activity in middle and secondary schools is the collection and indentification of soil samples. Such work can contribute to the study of biology, geography, environmental and local studies. The following program is based on a flowchart worksheet used in the local studies course at Bishop Wand School, Sunbury.

Rules are given describing the distinguishing characterization of particular types of soil. A sample is likely to be sand if it has a gritty consistency and it does not leave a dirty stain on the fingers.

x type sand if x consistency gritty and
                    not x leaves dirty-stain-on-fingers

> x type sandy-loan if x consistency gritty and
> x leaves dirty-stain-on-fingers and
> x moulds-into-ball

The information about the particular samples is to be provided by the user in response to questions. CHIMP will automatically ask the user when it does not know how to deal with a particular problem in the identification.

The point of the original flow-chart was to establish one identification for each sample. Once an identification has been made, the search can stop. Our rule to that effect uses the internal syntax of micro-PROLOG and the '!' symbol to restrict the search:

> x identity y if ! (type x y)

We have found a particular sample of soil. Here is the interaction which leads to its identification. We ask:

> which (x: sample1 identity x)

and the system responds with a series of questions:

> is (sample1 consistency gritty)? (yes/no) no
> is (sample1 feels silky)? (yes/no) yes
> is (sample1 moulds-into ball)? (yes/no) no
> is (sample1 will-polish between-thumb-and-finger)? (yes/no) no
> ===⟩ silty-loam
> No (more) answers

CHIMP (Child-oriented Interactive micro-PROLOG) is available for small micro-computers in educational use, and offers a more sophisticated form of the Query-the-user facility than is provided in the TOLD module provided with micro-PROLOG.

11.9 BIRD IDENTIFICATION PROGRAM (USING CHIMP)

Several classes have developed their own systems for identifying birds and other animals, using CHIMP in the classroom as a tool for building up an interactive classification system. They have visited their science resources centres to see what systems are described in their textbooks and other materials. One such is the 'Key to common birds in town gardens', on pages 10–11 of *Activities for young naturalists* by V. E. Graham (Hulton, 1969). This program represents the information from that key, rendering it accessible for interactive use.

The first question raised in the key concerns size. Two groups are described: "Pigeon size or larger" and "Smaller than a pigeon". We use two rules in PROLOG:

> x size large if x pigeon-size-or-larger
> x size small if not x pigeon-size-or-larger

Small birds are further classified, for example:

> x group titsize if x size small and
> x very-small

> x group sparrowsize if x size small and
> x colour black

Some birds are classified again into subgroups, for example:

> x subgroup redbreast if x groups sparrowsize and
> x breast pink-or-red

Each bird is then described in terms of its own distinguishing characteristics within a particular goup or subgroup, for example:

> x type rook if x group largeblack and
> x base-of-beak bare

> x type jackdaw if x group largeblack and
> x back-of-head grey and
> x eyes pale

> x type robin if x subgroup redbreast and
> x upper-parts dull-brown and
> x breast orange-red and
> x lower-parts white

The system is intended to be used to help in the identification of birds seen by the users. Each bird can only be of one type. We can express this in the rule:

> x identity y if ! (type x y)

All we have provided so far is a set of rules, and the user is required to provide further facts in answer to questions posed by the system. CHIMP automatically asks questions when it has no facts or rules concerning a relation.

This simple interaction illustrates the way in which the user works collaboratively with the system to solve the identification problem. We have seen a bird fly past, which we call Joey. What type of bird is he? We ask:

> which (x: Joey identity x)

In order to answer, the system poses a series of questions:

> is (Joey pigeon-size-or-larger)? (yes/no) no
> is (Joey very-small)? (yes/no) no
> is (Joey sparrow-size)? (yes/no) yes
> is (Joey cap black)? (yes/no) no
> is (Joey wings yellow-on)? (yes/no) no
> is (Joey tail long)? (yes/no) no
> is (Joey breast pink-or-red)? (yes/no) yes
> is (Joey upper-parts dull-brown)? (yes/no) yes
> is (Joey breast orange-red)? (yes/no) yes
> is (Joey lower-parts white)? (yes/no) yes
> ===) robin
> No (more) answers

The system has kept a record of the interaction:

> You denied the following
> Joey pigeon-size-or-larger
> You denied the following
> Joey very-small
> You confirmed the following
> Joey sparrow-size
> You denied the following
> Joey cap black
> You denied the following
> Joey wings yellow-on
> You denied the following
> Joey tail red
> Joey tail long
> You confirmed the following
> Joey breast pink-or-red
> Joey breast orange-red
> You confirmed the following
> Joey upper-parts dull-brown
> You confirmed the following
> Joey lower-parts white

Using the record of this interaction, we can obtain a summary taxonomy for Joey:

> one (x: Joey taxonomy x)
> ===⟩ (small sparrowsize redbreast robin)

11.10 DIET PROGRAM

One way of losing weight is to keep a close watch on the calories in the food we eat. Many people make reference to published guides, such as the *Doctor's quick weight loss diet* used in this program. The calorific content is listed for the appropriate quantity of a particular food. For example:

> (Bacon fried crisp 2 slices) calories 95
> (Beef roast lean 4oz) calories 210
> (Beef Hamburger lean grilled 4oz) calories 245

We can find out about the calorific content of various kinds of a particular food, for example cheese:

> which (x: Cheese cal x)
> (70 for (Cheddar 1 in cube))
> (30 for (Cottage creamed 1oz))
> (105 for (Cream 1oz))
> (105 for (Process 1oz))

(105 for (Roquefort 1oz)
(105 for (Swiss 1oz)
No (more) answers

If we have limited resources, we can enquire about means of cooking. What can be grilled, for example?

which (x: x can-be grilled)
Beef
Beef
Chicken
Turkey
Lamb
Veal
Mackerel
No (more) answers

Let us start to plan our meal:

What is the calorie content of the different meat and poultry dishes?
which (x y: x type meat-and-poultry and x calories y)

What desserts and sweets are available?
which (x: x type desserts-sweets)

We can describe what a slimming meal should be. It should contain three items, all different, whose total calorie value should be less than 500. We can add a rule:

(x y z) slimming-meal if   x calories X and
                            y calories Y and
                            z calories Z and
                            (x y z) all-different and
                            (X Y Z) sums-to x1 and
                            x1 LESS 500

Let us ask for suggestions for slimming meals containing chicken:

which (x: x slimming-meal and x contains Chicken)
((Bacon fried crisp 2 slices) (Beef roast lean 4oz) (Chicken grilled 3oz))
((Bacon fried crisp 2 slices) (Bologna sausage 4 in medium slice per slice) (Chicken grilled 3oz))
((Bacon fried crisp 2 slices) (Bologna sausage 4 in medium slice per slice) Chicken drumstick and thigh with bone fried 5oz))

We are given details of numerous slimming-meals, but most of them seem rather unbalanced. We should probably insist on some meat and poultry or fish and shellfish, some fruit or vegetable, and leave the third element open to choice. We can add a rule to check the balance of a meal:

(x y z) balanced-meal if   x course main and
                           y course side and
                           z course dessert

We can then relate these courses to the types in which our food items were classified:

x course main if x type meat-and-poultry
x course main if x type fish-and-shellfish
x course side if x type vegetables
x course side if x type fruits
x course dessert if x type desserts-sweets
x course dessert if x type diary-products-eggs-fats-oils-dressings
x course dessert if x type breads-and-grain-products

We can directly ask for a choice of balanced meals:

which (x: x balanced-meal)
((Bacon fried crisp 2 slices) (Asparagus medium each) Biscuits
                                      sweet average each))

We can also ask the more demanding question:

which (x: x balanced-meal and x slimming-meal)

which requests those meals that are both balanced and slimming.
    Finally, I would like to find a balanced slimming meal that allows me to have beef:

one (x: x balanced-meal and x with Beef and x slimming-meal)
((Beef roast lean 4oz) (Asparagus medium each) (Biscuits sweet
                                      average each))

more? (y/n)

Readers will note that in our Marseilles restaurant we could not order a slimming meal that contained beef.

11.11 CREATIVE WRITING PROGRAM

This program, originally developed with John Latham of Bishop Wand School, Sunbury, was produced to help motivate creative descriptive writing. In exploring extensions of a simple descriptive sentence, such as 'the house stood in a valley', by adding adjectives, adverbs, adjectival phrases, adverbial phrases, and prepositional phrases, as well as alternative nouns, verbs, and determiners, issues of syntax and grammar arise in a natural context.
    A sentence is defined as a nounphrase followed by a verbphrase:

x sentence if y nounphrase and
             z verbphrase and
             APPEND (y z x)

To cut our needlessly repetitive sentences, an 'oksentence' has been defined:

x oksentence if x sentence and
               not y repeated-on x

Nounphrase can take a number of rooms, with varying degrees of elaboration of description:

x nounphrase if x noun

x nounphrase if y determiner and
               z noun and
               APPEND (y z x)

x nounphrase if y determiner and
               z adjective and
               X noun and
               three-APPEND (y z X x)

x nounphrase if y determiner and
               z adjective and
               X adjective and
               Y noun and
               four-APPEND (y z X Y x)

x nounphrase if y determiner and
               z noun and
               X adjectival-phase and
               three-APPEND (y z X x)

Similarly verbphrases can vary in form, depending on the degree of description and on the presence of a nounphrase:

x verbphrase if x verb

x verbphrase if y verb and
               z abverb and
               APPEND (y z x)

x verbphrase if y verb and
               z preposition and
               X nounphrase and
               three-APPEND (y z X x)

x verbphrase if y verb and
               z adverb and
               X preposition and
               y nounphrase and
               four-APPEND (y z X Y x)

We are not just concerned with issues of syntax. Our choice of vocabulary will determine the mood and meaning of our sentences within syntactic framework. We regard a sentence as expressing a particular mood if the nounphrase and verbphase express that mood:

x sentence-mood y if z nounphrase-mood y and
                      X verbphrase-mood y and
                      APPEND (z X x)

We can check the mood of a nounphrase or verbphrase by checking the mood of all their descriptive words, their adjectives, adjectival phrases, adverbs, and adverbial phrases.

x nounphrase-mood y if x nounphrase and
                        (forall z ON x and
                            (either z adjective
                             or z adjectival-phrase)
                        then z mood y)
x verbphrase-mood y if x verbphrase and
                        (forall z ON x and
                            (either z adverb
                             or z adverbial-phrase)
                        then z mood y) and
                        (forall X on x and
                            (either X adjective
                             or X adjectival-phrase)
                        then X mood y)

In the questions that follow we use the following vocabulary:

(house) noun
(valley) noun
(dark) adjective
(gloomy) adjective
(deserted) adjective
(alone) adverb
(in) preposition
(near) preposition
(showing no signs of human occupation) adjectival-phrase
(defiantly hostile) adverbial-phrase
(a) determiner
(the) determiner

Each of the adjectives, adverbs, adjectival phrases, and adverbial phrases is described as nasty in mood.

The same vocabulary and rules can be used to both check the correctness of given sentences and to generate sentences.

which (x: x oksentence)
(house stood)
(house stood alone)

(house stood in valley)
(house stood in a valley)
(house stood in the dark valley)
(house stood in the gloomy valley)
(house stood in the deserted valley)
(house stood in a dark valley)
(house stood in a gloomy valley)
(house stood in the dark gloomy valley)
(house stood in the dark deserted valley)
. . .
(house stood alone near the valley showing no signs of human occupation)
. . .
(the house stood in a valley showing no signs of human occupation)
. . .
(the dark house stood in a gloomy deserted valley)
. . .
(the gloomy house stood alone in a valley showing no signs of human
occupation)
. . .
(a dark deserted house stood alone near the valley showing no signs of
human occupation)
. . .
is ((the deserted valley) nounphrase)
YES
is ((stood in the dark valley) verbphrase-mood nasty)
YES
is ((the deserted house stood alone in a gloomy valley) oksentence)
YES
is ((the house stood alone) sentence)
YES
which (x: x mood nasty)
(defiantly hostile)
(dark)
(alone)
(gloomy)
(showing no signs of human occupation)
(deserted)
No (more) answers

12

The importance of PROLOG

12.1 INTRODUCTION

PROLOG (PROgramming in LOGic) represents a major advance towards a longer-term objective of logic programming. It is a programming language in its own right, available in numerous implementations around the world since the first implementation in Marseilles in 1972. It was chosen by the Japanese Fifth Generation Computer Systems researchers as the fundamental starting point in their development of a new generation of computer systems. It is being applied internationally in research areas such as databases, expert systems, natural language understanding, software engineering and specification. Despite the range of research uses, the available literature remains somewhat limited, particularly regarding issues of teaching PROLOG programming.

In this chapter we try to examine the importance of PROLOG in the context of teaching computing. We try to draw on the diversity of approaches and traditions that already exist in the field of logic programming and its applications.

First we need to look briefly at the research and academic tradition from which PROLOG developed. More properly we should say that PROLOG comes from a number of traditions, that in fact it already has several histories.

12.2 THE TRADITION OF NATURAL LANGUAGE PROCESSING

Alain Colmerauer, leader of the group in Marseilles that first implemented PROLOG, had worked in Montreal for several years on problems of machine translation, and was particularly influenced by the work of Chomsky in linguistics. He and his colleagues were exploring ways of dealing with human natural languages and with computer languages on computers, with ideas of compiling from one language to another applying in both cases.

A number of new experimental languages were developed by the researchers in Montreal and Marseilles. One was the language "TARZAN – a language for manipulating trees", of which little more has been heard. Colmerauer worked with Henry Kanoui, Phillipe Roussel, and Robert Pasero. Roussel was concerned with the deductive part of their experimental system, and explored the possible use of logic. Robert Kowalski worked with Colmerauer from 1972, both in Marseilles and Edinburgh. Colmerauer's group has developed a series of implementations of PROLOG for mainframes, minicomputers, and microcomputers, and has continued to be largely concerned with natural language understanding and translation. Why should Frenchmen have to communicate with each other or with computers in any language other than God's chosen language, French?

12.3 THE TRADITION OF LOGIC

Kowalski came to his collaboration with Colmerauer from a very different background. He was particularly concerned with logical reasoning. Natural language contains numerous areas of imprecision and ambiguity, which can often lead to misunderstanding. In contrast he saw formal logic as offering a model of clarity and precision. Kowalski's early writings concern particular approaches to problem solving and theorem proving. He was much influenced by the work of Alan Robinson on 'resolution', a way of using computers to draw logical inferences, and he focused his own attention on a particular form of logic known as 'Horn clauses' (named after Alfred Horn, a German logician). While Colmerauer and his group implemented PROLOG for natural language applications, Kowalski was concerned with the theory of logic programming, which he has developed in a long series of papers and an influential book *Logic for Problem Solving,* published in 1979.

12.4 THE TRADITION OF IMPLEMENTATION

The third tradition to note in the development of PROLOG is that of implementation. The work of David Warren, in particular, has been crucial to the proliferation and practical use of PROLOG. It was his work on the widely-used Edinburgh DEC-10 PROLOG that produced a compiler that can rival the other principal AI language, LISP, in speed. This has enabled researchers to build large efficient systems with today's computers. It was Warren's DEC-10 PROLOG that was taken by the Japanese as their starting point for their development of logic programming kernel languages. At Imperial College, Keith Clark and Frank McCabe developed extensions to DEC-10 PROLOG in their IC-PROLOG. Clark and Steve Gregory have continued, developing PARLOG, a parallel logic programming language. Many of their ideas are used in Ehud Shapiro's Concurrent PROLOG and the Japanese kernel languages. At the other extreme, McCabe's implementation of micro-PROLOG makes PROLOG available on the whole range of microcomputers. PROLOG is no longer confined to the research laboratory, but is available wherever there are computers.

12.5 PROLOG AND LOGIC PROGRAMMING

If we look around the present community of researchers and users of PROLOG and logic programming, we can identify different emphases, long-term objectives, and current approaches to introducing PROLOG. In particular we can distinguish between those whose prime concern is the efficient use of today's PROLOG as a programming language, with no interest in research or theory, and those for whom PROLOG is merely a step on the way to logic programming.

In this chapter we are concerned with the importance of PROLOG, as a new 'computer language', in learning about computing in general and programming in particular. At the present time, when the nature of computers and the activity of programming are changing, logic programming and PROLOG are extremely important, whether or not the individual trained programmer eventually finds himself required to program in PROLOG. The director of the Japanese Fifth Generation project, in a lighter moment, once wrote that "soon even cats and spoons will program in PROLOG". We do not have to take that literally.

12.6 LOGIC PROGRAMMING AS A MARTIAL ART

We can learn something by exploring the spirit in which the Japanese researchers have taken to the disciplines of logic programming. In a recent article (Murakami, 1983) called 'Archery discipline and Fifth Generation computer research', Kunio Murakami, chief of the First Laboratory at ICOT (The Institute for New Generation Computing) wrote about logic programming as a new kind of 'martial art':

> "Japanese arts and martial arts place an extreme importance on discipline. Discipline originally means to study things form the past in order to apply them to the current world, as well as to imitate procedures and forms established by predecessors in order to master the essence of the individual arts. Without getting the knack of an art, no one can show true originality. In fact a number of trainees mastered the secret of an art with this approach and took a new step towards originality by establishing new schools, surpassing the level which their predecessors had reached."

The first stage of the Japanese project placed a lot of emphasis on learning from overseas masters of the new art: and many of the founding figures of logic programming have been guests at ICOT, including Robinson, Kowalski, Colmerauer, Warren, Shapiro, Clark, and Gregory mentioned above.

12.7 LOGIC PROGRAMMING + FUNCTIONAL
PROGRAMMING = ASSERTIONAL PROGRAMMING

Alan Robinson, as the 'godfather' of logic programming, has tried to identify its most important elements, both for ICOT and a wider audience. He talks of logic programming and functional programming together as 'assertional programming'. In simple terms, assertional programming is:

"a type of programming in which what you do is assert some sentences to be true, and then ask for others to be deduced as a consequence."

This contrasts very clearly with conventional programming, where what you do is give a series of instructions to a machine.

12.8 A DECLARATIVE APPROACH

In this book, and in work in logic programming influenced by the approach at Imperial College, we have tried to use logic descriptively, describing the information with which we are concerned. We also want to emphasize the declarative style of programming. The user's description of his problem constitutes the program, with no particular order imposed on facts or conditions in rules. The computer system should have the 'intelligence' to provide further facilities for the user, such as allowing him to describe the kind of output that he wants, and to use graphics. The user can give a 'declarative reading' to each sentence of his program, independent of the way the program is to be used by the computer.

The approach is independent of a particular computer archietecture. In a description of a problem, or in a list of conditions for a rule, the order of the answers to a question does not matter logically. It does not matter logically if one processor or many hundreds of processors are involved. The same program should run on a vast variety of machines.

A section of the British Alvey Research Programme in Advanced Information Technology is devoted to 'Declarative Systems Architecture', where declarative languages such as PROLOG are taken as a focus for designing future computer architectures. The majority of today's large-scale applications programs using DEC-10 PROLOG have been more conventional and procedural, more dependent on the design of today's machines.

12.9 LOGIC PROGRAMMING FOR BEGINNERS

Beginners come to logic programming from a wide range of backgrounds. We can start, as we have done in this book, with describing subjects that are familiar to the individual learner, or use logic programming to help in the teaching of other subjects. Some beginners are better than others in learning to generalize and to deal with abstraction, but all can gain understanding by describing problems known to them, and gradually modifying their prototype description until it meets their requirements.

12.10 LOGIC AND PROGRAMMING SKILLS

The declarative use of logic provides a number of benefits in the learning of programming. We are emphasizing the development of a problem description or specification. Specifications are often written in logic, without the writer being worried about how efficiently that will be handled by the computer. We can construct a rapid prototype of a complex system in PROLOG, and test and modify it before final construction, either in PROLOG or some other language that might be more appropriate for the application. It is natural to develop PROLOG programs top-down, encouraging approaches to problem decomposition and structure.

12.11 LOGIC AND COMPUTER SCIENCE

Some familiarity with the notation of predicate logic, used in PROLOG, made easier by using it for executable programs, is an advantage in many areas of computer science. Work in the field of databases has involved logic and relational databases for some years, and a variety of query systems have been developed using PROLOG and other logical notations. In AI there has been a long controversy over the role of logic, many researchers having dimissed practical applications of theorem provers in the 1960s. Predicate logic is very powerful for representing knowledge, and, given the long tradition of using rules ('production rules') for carrying out inferences in expert systems, it is not surprising that PROLOG is itself used both for knowledge representation and for carrying out the inferences in expert systems. This considerably simplifies the design of such systems. In natural language translation and understanding logic is one of the favoured notations, and from simple examples one can progress to advanced translation systems.

12.12 LOGIC PROGRAMMING AND SOFTWARE ENGINEERING

Relations between logic programmers and software engineers have perhaps been uneasy. A view has been expressed that today's problems of software engineering will to a large extent be solved by fifth generation systems with automatic programming and applications generation facilities. At present both logic programmers and software engineers share concern for problems of scale, complexity, and consistency, and PROLOG is one of the tools used by software engineers for prototyping and system development.

12.13 LOGIC PROGRAMMING AND NEW COMPUTER ARCHITECTURES

PROLOG is very amenable to adaptation to parallel machines. A number of links have been developing between logic programming and functional programming at this level, and new languages are emerging that are amalgamations of the two notations. Machines such as the ALICE machine at Imperial College, designed for functional languages, will also support PROLOG, PARLOG, and other logic programming languages. PROLOG machines are being built in Japan, along the lines of LISP machines, designed to fit the requirements of the particular languages. PROLOG also runs on LISP machines, and on new machines such as the Abstract PROLOG Machine (APM) that also supports functional languages. Many new parallel logic programming architectures are under development, such as Shapiro's 'Bagel'.

12.14 WHERE DOES THE USER FIT IN? WHAT DOES HE NEED TO KNOW?

It may be that programming and computer science in general are at a turning point, and this must affect not only today's practitioners but today's learners. Computers are no longer scarce resources, and offer more power at a lower price than could have been predicted. We need to consider afresh the place of computers and what should be taught.

The British Alvey Report was critical of the spread of microcomputers accompanied by the bad habits of the 1950s and 1960s, which are producing further generations of poor BASIC programmers. It said that languages should be chosen with an eye to the future.

It does not seem likely that in the future we will require the present balance of programmer skills. Parallel computers and applications generators will place different requirements on the user and programmer. The programmer as we know him today, spending long hours over lines of code, may become redundant, his craft rendered obsolete by the advance of information technology.

Hand-loom weavers and programmers

It is tempting to pursue the parallel with the hand-loom workers whose productivity and efficiency could not rival that of the new power looms. Many of them, distressed by the change in their personal circumstances from a position of security and prosperity, took direct physical action against the new machines on which they blamed their fate. Their most famous leader was Ned Ludd. Readers will recall that the punched cards used by Jacquard to control his looms, giving instructions as to what patterns should be followed by the machine, were adapted by Hollerith, founder of IBM, for recording census data. Increasingly, work in advanced computing and artificial intelligence has concerned patterns at different levels, and programs can take on many tasks for which human expertise was previously essential.

A whole industry of home and office workers in software, a cottage industry whose products are of variable quality and whose workers had little formal training, learning on the job, may be threatened. It has certainly been true in recent years that 'Luddite' reactions to new generation computing ideas have been most pronounced from those most wedded to current ways of working in the computer industry. If that is so, then the implications for education, training, and economic policy are enormous.

A fifth-generation computer is intended to understand natural language voice input: the computer user will not be required to learn high-level computer language. The intelligent user will need skills in declarative and procedural styles of thinking that are more related to the subject-matter of his 'intelligent knowledge-based system' than to the machine on which it is implemented. Our students now in schools and colleges will be the users of those fifth-generation computers. First, however, the computers must be built. In the meantime, the future users can acquire the thinking skills using today's machines.

12.15 PROBLEMS WITH LOGIC PROGRAMMING AND PROLOG

There are distinct problems and dangers. The approach to computing taken by logic programmers differs from the traditional view. It can be hard for a student steeped in conventional procedural ways of thinking to grasp the declarative concepts of logic programming, yet the novice finds a declarative approach natural and straightforward. Computer science has need of both procedural and declarative approaches. It is becoming progressively more difficult to find students not already adversely affected by their experience with BASIC, still open to a fresh start. Governments in their rush to modernize and adopt information technology may have seriously damaged their chances of long-term success by proliferating ill-considered computing courses. Even high-level programming languages like PASCAL can hinder the development of declarative thinking needed for program specification.

Problems have also arisen through over-enthusiasm: logic programmers have been regarded as claiming too much, too soon. PROLOG implementations are widespread and powerful, but many problems remain. Expectations have been raised, research projects abound, but these things take time. The Japanese Fifth Generation Project is working on a ten-year timescale during which there is no obligation on them to produce commercial products. The basis of funding of British, European, and American research tends to be shorter-term, and companies are more preoccupied with commercial survival. Some of these differences are lessening with greater international collaboration between companies, research groups, and governments, and with increased realization by governments of the nature of the problems to be overcome.

An earlier version of this chapter was published in "The Role of Programming in Teaching Informatics" eds Griffiths M, Tagg E. D. North-Holland 1985.

13

History, computers, and logical reasoning: today and tomorrow

Readers will have noticed a contrast between what has been described as the promise of computers as aids in the study and teaching of historical issues, and the examples of programs developed to date as illustrations in the different chapters. In this concluding chapter I would like to analyse some of the weaknesses of the work I have described, and to explore the ways in which we can expect improvements in the future.

There are a number of obvious limitations on work in this field, particularly when applied to the educational system. Schools and colleges have access to microcomputers, often in great numbers, but normally with limited memory capacity. Artificial Intelligence languages such as PROLOG, LISP, LOGO, POP, and SMALLTALK depend on large memories for really effective working, as do Intelligent Tutoring Systems. In theory this is becoming less of a problem, as the cost of computer memory falls, but ill-financed educational institutions in the United Kingdom are slow to replace one generation of microcomputers with another. The speed of change in this respect is greater in the United States and Australia. On small machines we can give a taste of what lies ahead, but the constraints of space, at least for researchers, are no longer an excuse for limited imagination in applications programs.

Another limitation has been the use of the QWERTY keyboard as the sole means of input, meaning that the user has had to master the keyboard as well as non-natural language conventions in order to communicate with the computer. Already this is becoming an avoidable problem, as alternative forms of input are used in education. The Concept Keyboard allows use to be made of pictures, colours, or symbols instead of letters or words if desired. A technological extension of this more 'iconic' approach can be seen in the increasingly popular menu systems, touch-sensitive screens, and sophisticated programming environments controlled by a hand-held 'mouse', on computers such as the LISA and Macintosh, doubtless to be followed by the more powerful full SMALLTALK environment. The whole area of man-machine interaction is the subject of considerable research, and facilities for the user can increasingly be tailored to suit his requirements in the context of the application.

In earlier chapters I have made reference to work in natural language processing, which has been the prime application area studied by many researchers with PROLOG, including Colmerauer's orginal team in Marseilles. David Warren and Fernando Pereira demonstrated with their CHAT-80 system the power of PROLOG in translating questions in English into queries in logic and obtaining the answers in an efficient manner from large databases of facts and rules. Large parts of that system can be run with PROLOG implementations addressing 128K of memory, and certainly with the spread of powerful workstations based on the 68000 microprocessor it is becoming viable to have both a substantial database and a sophisticated natural language 'front end' program. If we examine the new personal PROLOG machines under development in the United Kingdom, the United States, and Japan, and the new parallel computers such as ALICE, under development at Imperial College, it seems likely that massive increases in cost offer enormous possibilities. In Japan, large teams of researchers are working on natural language understanding systems, working from text or spoken input.

In the near future we are likely to be offered systems that can understand typed input of natural language in a given subject domain, so long as we avoid the most complex grammatical constructions. There are greater problems in understanding spoken language or an unrestricted subject domain, not least that of grasping the context of what is being said. This problem is being addressed by AI researchers including Jon Barwise of Stanford, with his theories of situation semantics, as well as, of course, the Japanese.

Educational applications and historical research have not been prime areas of government-funded or commercially-funded support. Many researchers have thus been obliged to work in different application fields, reducing the base of expertise available to assist teachers, lecturers, and students. Conventional advice and lecturing on the educational use of computers has drawn little on the AI tradition, and has continued to emphasize traditional computer-assisted learning and the use of languages such as BASIC. This continues to alienate teachers of subjects such as history.

As I argued in the opening chapter, I see the way forward with computers in terms of clearer reflection on the past. Developing computer technology offers us an unprecedented opportunity for exploring issues of a complexity and degree of abstraction that otherwise defy consideration. To take an example from my own research group, a complex statistical modelling system has been implemented in FORTRAN for a number of years. Under a project now beginning, an 'intelligent front end program' is to be developed in PROLOG, allowing the user conversational interaction with the model, including explanations for conclusions that are reached. In an earlier chapter I gave a simple example of a Keynesian model of the deflationary economic spiral, which could be made to operate in response to questions. On a larger scale we should expect 'intelligent front ends' to the Treasury model of the economy, Government, and Local Authority policy models, and international population models.

In straightforward terms, we can see ourselves not only as entitled to explanations of complex problems or obscure decisions, but as equipped with tools that can help us to obtain such explanations. We require from an expert system the level of explanation and clarity that we require but all too rarely receive from human experts.

We can only obtain explanations if there is information, or evidence, available for us to use. Crucially, we can only use it if we know how to deal with evidence, what questions to ask, what generalisations we can sensibly induce from given evidence. These are the concerns of history, and of teachers of history particularly those working in the traditions of the 'new history' that emphasizes the methods and procedures of the historian. Historians are accustomed to working with incomplete information, piecing together a picture from scattered fragments, to the extent that for an historian the idea of having all the evidence, complete knowledge of a particular real-life problem, does not make sense. His aim is to arrive at a coherent understanding of a problem, reconciling apparent conflicts in information from different sources. For the historian a problem understood is a problem solved. The problem may not stay solved, as new evidence may come to light that forces the historian to reconsider his view. In one sense, the same problem may have several different solutions over time, as the evidence perceived as relevant changes and new assessments are made, perhaps by different historians. In another sense, each time it is a different problem, or described differently.

Complex systems, such as companies, legislation or regulations, or governments, could be open to scrutiny. Freedom of information legislation in different countries is intended to facilitate that process. Official Secrets Acts are intended to frustrate it, denying information to the questioner, and penalizing the official who answers the awkward question. I have outlined in earlier chapters a model of collaborative problem solving, where knowledge is pooled to aid in the solution of a problem that is beyond the understanding of the individual inquirer. Where answers are denied, collaboration breaks down. There may of course be powerful reasons why certain information may not be divulged, and a trained historian can discern such 'reasons for action'. Such secrecy may be frustrating to the historian, but not incomprehensible, for he may be familiar with the life and writings of Machiavelli, author of *The Prince*, an 'expert system' of advice for Renaissance princes.

Historians have experience in the domain of what are being called 'belief systems' from which we can learn, with the aid of our collaborative problem-solving model. Scientists often have the urge to explain everything, in the sense of developing a free-standing working model of a system and how it works. Historians need to describe how things are, in such a way that a coherent account is given, from which explanations of answers to questions can be given in terms of other parts of the description, rather than from some underlying reductionist model. In this sense, within the closed world of a belief system, the process of question and answer described by Collingwood will come to a halt, not just with:

No (more) answers

but with the corollary in this model of explanation:

No (more) questions

There is no doubt that in the educational use of computers in history teaching, the classroom teacher of history has made most productive use of the technology if he has refused to compromise his expert view of the subject. This point can be generalized and reversed. An expert system will have an educational or training potential value directly related to the extent to which it embodies real expertise, worthy of application and explanation. We should see systems developed by experts for work in their fields as potential teaching tools. The expert systems developed by the French social historians and social scientists whose work was quoted earlier in the book could provide excellent teaching tools for the 'new history', where history is taught as a way of thinking.

We should be approaching the position where we can offer paradigms for the use of AI techniques in history teaching, to form a vital part of the imaginative advance of the subject. This book is a contribution towards that end, and stems from the realization that the underlying concerns of AI and history teaching are similar. Before the term 'artificial intelligence' had been coined, R. G. Collingwood described history as "the science of mind". Is it too much to hope that the sharing of insights can continue?

References

Abelson, R. P. (1973) 'The structure of belief systems' in: eds Schank, R. & Colby, *Computer models of thought and language,* Freeman.

Abelson, H. & Di Sessa, A. (1981) *Turtle geometry: the computer as a medium for exploring mathematics.* MIT Press.

Alpert, D. & Bitzer, D. L. (1970) 'Advances in computer-based education' *Science* 20 March 1970 1582–1590.

Alvey (1982) The Report of the Alvey Committee, *A programme for advanced information technology,* Department of Industry, London.

Austin, J. L. (1962) *How to do things with words,* Oxford Univ. Press.

Ayer, A. J. (1946) *Language, truth and logic,* Gollancz.

Bannister, D. (1970) (ed.) *Perspectives in personal construct theory,* Academic Press.

Bannister, D. & Fransella, F. (1971) *Inquiring man* Penguin.

Barnes, J. A. (1954) 'Class and committees in a Norwegian parish' *Human Relations* **vii** (No. 1) 43.

Batani, G. & Meloni, H. (1973) *Interpreteur du langage de programmation PROLOG,* Groupe Intelligence Artificielle, Univ of Aix-Marseille, Luminy.

Bhaskar, R. (1978) *A realist theory of science,* Harvester.

Birt, D. & Nichol, J. (1975) *Games and simulations in history,* Longman.

Borillo, M. (1981) 'A Propos des Bases de Donnees: sur le role des sciences de l'homme dans le developpement de l'informatique', in: eds Chouraqui, E. & Virbel, J. *Banques d'informations dans les sciences de l'homme monographics d'informatique de l'AFCET* Editions Hommes et Technique.

Boden, M. (1977) *Artificial intelligence and natural man,* Harvester.

Boden, M. (1979) *Piaget,* Fontana.

Boomer, Garth (1983a) *Zen and the art of computing* Wattle Park Teachers Centre, South Australia.

Boomer, Garth (1983b) *Towards a science of English teaching*, Wattle Park Teachers Centre, South Australia.

Booth, M. (1969) *History betrayed* Longman.

Booth, M. (1978) 'Inductive thinking in history: the 14–16 age group, in: eds Jones, G. & Ward, L. *New history, old problems*, Swansea.

Du Boulay, B. (1979) 'Teaching teachers mathematics through programming' *DAI Research Paper*, No. 113, Univ. Edinburgh.

Du Boulay, B. & O'Shea, T. (1980) 'Teaching novices programming' *DAI Research paper*, No. 132 University of Edinburgh, and in: ed Coombs, M. *Computing skills and adaptive systems*, Academic Press.

Du Boulay, B. & Howe, J. A. M. (1981) 'Re-learning mathematics through LOGO: helping student teachers who don't understand mathematics, in: eds Howe, J. A. M. & Ross, P. *Microcomputers in secondary education*, Kogan Page.

Bowen, K. (1982) 'Programming with full first-order logic', in: eds Hayes, J. E., Michie, D., Pao, Y. H. *Machine intelligence 10*, Ellis Horwood.

Bowen, K. & Kowalski, R. A. (1982) 'Amalgamating language and metalanguage in logic programming', in: eds Clark, K. L. & Tarnlund, S-A. *Logic Programming*, Academic Press.

Bramer, M. (1984) 'The Japanese fifth generation computer project' in ed: Burns, A. *New information technology*, Ellis Horwood.

Briggs, J. H. (1982) 'Teaching mathematics with PROLOG'. BSc thesis, Dept. of Computing, Imperial College.

Briggs, J. H. (1983) *PROLOG for cryptography*, Dept. of Computing, Imperial College.

Briggs, J. H. (1984a) *Designing and implementing a child-orientated interface to micro-PROLOG*, Dept. of Computing, Imperial College.

Briggs, J. H. (1984b) *Applying logic programming techniques to history teaching*, Dept. of Computing, Imperial College.

Briggs, J. H. (1984) *micro-PROLOG rules!* Logic Programming Associates.

Brough, D. R. (1982) *Loop Trapping for children's Logic Programs Logic Working Paper*, 10 Dept. of Computing, Imperial College.

Brough, D. R. (1984) 'micro-PROLOG for problem-solving', in: ed Ramsden, E. *Microcomputers in Education 2*, Ellis Horwood.

Brown, J. S., Burton, R. R., & Bell, A. G. (1975) 'SOPHIE: a step towards creating a reactive learning environment', *Int. J. Man-Machine Studies*, 7, 675–696.

Bruner, J. S. (1968) 'The course of cognitive growth', in: eds Wason, P. & Johnson-Laird, *Thinking and reasoning*, Penguin.

Bruner, J. S. (1972) *The relevance of education*, George Allen & Unwin.

Bruner, J. S., Goodnow, J. J. & Austin, G. A. (1956) *A study of thinking*, John Wiley.

Bruner, J. S. & Kenney, H. J. (1968) 'Representation and mathematics learning', in: eds Wason, P. & Johnson-Laird, *Thinking and reasoning*, Penguin.

Bryant, P. L. (1977) 'Logical inferences and development', in: Geber, B. A. *Piaget and knowing*, Routledge Kegan Paul.

Buchanan, B. G. & Feigenbaum, E. A. (1978) 'Dendral and metaDendral: their applications dimension', in: *Atrificial Intelligence 11*.

Bundy, A. (ed) (1978) *Artificial intelligence: an introductory course,* Edinburgh Univ. Press.

Bundy, A. (1981) 'Mental machines rule OK' *DAI Occasional Paper,* No. 25, Univ. Edinburgh.

Bundy, A., Byrd, L., Luger, G., Mellish, C. & Palmer, M. (1979) 'Solving mechanics problems using meta-level inference', in: ed Michie, D. *Expert systems in the microelectronic age,* Edinburgh Univ. Press.

Buzbee, B. L., (198) Ewald, R. H. & Worlton, W. J. 'Japanese supercomputer technology' *Science,* **218,** 17 December 1982.

Carbonnel, J. R. (1970) 'AI in CAI: an artificial intelligence approach to computer-assisted instruction' *IEEE Transactions on Man-Machine Systems,* **MMS-11,** 190–202.

Carey, S. (1983) *PROLOG for the ITECS,* Information Technology Consultancy Unit, London.

Chamoux, A. (1979) 'Family reconstitution: hopes and realities' *Informatique et Histoire,* INRIA.

Chomsky, N. (1972) *Problems of knowledge and freedom,* Fontana.

Chouraqui, E. & Virbel, J. (eds) (1981) *Banques d'informations dans les sciences de l'homme monographies d'informatique de l'AFCER,* Editions Aemmes et Techniques.

Cicourel, A. V. (1964) *Method and measurement in sociology,* New York.

Clark, K. L., Ennals, J. R. & McCabe, F. G. (1981) *A micro-PROLOG primer* Logic Programming Associates.

Clark, K. L., McCabe, F. G., & Hammond, P. (1982) 'PROLOG: a language for implementing expert systems, in: eds Hayes, J. E., Michie, D., & Pao, Y. H. *Machine Intelligence 10,* Ellis Horwood.

Clark, K. L. & Gregory, S. (1982) *PARLOG: a relational language for parallel programming,* Dept. of Computing, Imperial College.

Clark, K. L. & Tarnlund, S-A. (eds) (1982) *Logic programming,* Academic Press.

Clark, K. L. & McCabe, F. G. (1984) *micro-PROLOG: programming in logic,* Prentice-Hall.

Clocksin, W. & Mellish, C. (1981) *Programming in PROLOG,* Springer-Verlag.

Colby, K. M. (1973) 'Simulations of belief systems', in: eds Schank, R. & Colby, K. M. *Computer models of thought and language,* Freeman.

Collingwood, R. G. (1939) *Autobiography,* Oxford Univ. Press.

Collingwood, R. G. (1946) *The idea of history,* Oxford Univ. Press.

Colmerauer, A. (1969) *Mechanical translation project report No. 12,* special edition on W-grammars, Univ. of Montreal.

Colmerauer, A. (1971) *Les systemes-Q ou un formalisme pour analyser et synthesier des phrases sur ordinateur,* Univ. de Montreal.

Colmerauer, A. (1978) *Metamorphosis grammars,* Springer-Verlag Notes on Computer Science.

Colmerauer, A. (1982) *PROLOG II reference manual and theoretical model,* Groupe Intelligence Artificielle, Univ. of Aix-Marseille, Luminy.

Cory, T., Hammond, P., Kowalski, R. A., Kriwaczek, F., Sadri, F., & Sergot, M. *The British Nationality Act as a logic program,* Dept. of Computing, Imperial College.

Cumming, G. (1983) *Logic programming and cognitive development,* La Trobe University, Melbourne.

Darlington, J. & Reeve, M. (1983) 'ALICE: a multi-processor reduction machine', in: *Proc Conf on Functional Programming Languages and Computer Architecture,* ACM New York.

Daniel, G. (1981) *A Short history of archaeology,* Thames & Hudson.

Davidson, D. (1968) 'Actions, reasons and causes', in: ed. White, A. R. *The philosophy of action,* Oxford Univ. Press.

Davidson, D. (1976) 'Psychology as philosophy', in: ed Glover, J. *The philosophy of mind,* Oxford Univ. Press.

Dickinson, A. & Lee, P. J. (eds) (1977) *History teaching and historical understanding,* Heinemann.

Dijkstra, E. W. (1972) 'Notes on structured programming', in: Dahl, O-J., Dijkstra, E. W., & Hoare, C. A. R. *Structured programming,* Academic Press.

Donaldson, M. (1978) *Children's minds,* Collins.

Doran, J. (1977) 'Knowledge representation for archaeological inference', in: eds Elcock, E. & Michie, D. *Machine Intelligence 8,* Ellis Horwood.

Doyle, J. (1980) 'A model for deliberation, action and introspection', *AI Technical Report 581,* MIT AI Lab, May 1980.

Dunn, J. (1969) *The political thought of John Locke,* Cambridge Univ. Press.

Dunn, J. (1972) *Modern Revolutions,* Cambridge Univ. Press.

Elias, N. (1971) Sociology of knowledge, *Sociology,* **5.**

Elton, G. R. (1969) *The practice of history,* Fontana.

Van Emden, M. (1977) 'Programming with resolution logic', in: eds. Elcock E. W. & Michie, D. *Machine Intelligence 8,* Ellis Horwood.

Ennals, J. R. (1979a) 'Historical Simulation' *Practical Computing,* July 1979.

Ennals, J. R. 'Involving the Student' *Practical Computing,* August 1979, and in: ed. Sledge, D. *Microcomputers in education,* CET (1979).

Ennals, J. R. (1979b) *The European Parliament in the classroom,* Essex European Resources Centre.

Ennals. J. R. (1980a) 'Simulations and computers', *Teaching History,* June 1980.

Ennals, J. R. (1981a) 'Some applications of logic and programming to the teaching of history', *History Teaching Review,* April 1981.

Ennals, J. R. (1981b) *Children program in PROLOG,* Dept. of Computing, Imperial College.

Ennals, J. R. (1981c) 'Logic as a computer language for children', *Educational Computing,* October 1981.

Ennals, J. R. (1981d) *Logic as a computer language for children: a one-year course,* Imperial College.

Ennals, J. R. (1981e) *History and computing: a collection of papers 1979–1981,* Imperial College DOC report 81/22.

Ennals, J. R. (1981f) 'Logic and Computing for Schools' *Practical Computing,* March 1982 (PROLOG can link diverse subjects with logic and fun).

Ennals, J. R. (1982a) 'History teaching and artificial intelligence, *Teaching History,* June 1982.

Ennals, J. R. (1982b) 'Teaching logic as a computer language in schools' *Proc. First International Logic Programming Conference Marseilles 1982* ed. Van Canegehem, M., and in: Yazdani, M. *New Horizons in educational computing,* Ellis Horwood, and in: eds. Warren, D. & Van Caneghem, M. *Logic programming and its applications,* Ablex.

Ennals, J. R. (1982c) 'Teaching logic as a computer language to children', *AISB Quarterly,* Autumn 1982.

Ennals, J. R. (1982d) *History and computing,* Dept. of Computing, Imperial College, and in: ed. Larsson, Y. *Bringing the past alive: history teaching in the eighties,* Allen & Unwin (forthcoming).

Ennals, J. R. (1982e) *Beginning micro-PROLOG,* Ellis Horwood and Heinemann. Second revised edition Ellis Horwood and Heinemann (1984) and Harper & Row (1984).

Ennals, J. R. (1982f) 'micro-PROLOG for historical simulation', *Practical Computing,* December 1982 (Revolution in education).

Ennals, J. R. (1983a) 'Artificial intelligence' in: ed. Rushby, N. J. *Computer-based learning,* Pergamon Infotech State of the Art Report.

Ennals, J. R. & Brough, D. R. (1982) 'Representing the expert knowledge of the archaeologists', in: *Proc. Computer Applications in Archaeology 1982,* Birmingham University, ed. Laflin, S.

Ennals, J. R. (1984a) *Beginning micro-PROLOG* (Second revised edition) Ellis Horwood and Heinemann (1984) and Harper & Row.

Ennals, J. R. (1984b) 'The importance of PROLOG', in "The Role of Programming in Teaching Informatics" eds Griffiths M, Tagg E. D. North-Holland 1985.

Ennals, J. R. (1984c) *Describing your world,* presented at Conference of National Association for teachers of English, Durham.

Ennals, J. R. (1984d) 'The use of the computer in the study and teaching of history: possibilities and priorities for the future', Historical Association Education Conference 1984 *'The use of the computer in the study and teaching of history'* report ed. Randell, K. Historical Association, and in: *Education, Telematique, Informatique,* No. 1 Feb 1984, Laboratoire d'Informatique pour les Sciences de l'Homme LISH-CNRS Paris.

Ennals, J. R. (1984e) 'Education for the future with computers', *Times Educational Supplement,* 2 March 1984.

Ennals, J. R. (1984f) 'Towards the future with micro-PROLOG', *Times Educational Supplement,* May 1984, and in: 'Read using' *Research Machines Users Magazine,* 1984.

Ennals, J. R. (1984g) 'micro-PROLOG for classroom historical research', in: *Education et Informatique,* Paris 1984 and in: eds. Reid, J., Rushton, J. *Teachers, Computers and the Classroom,* Manchester University Press, 1985.

Ennals, J. R. (1984h) 'The promise of intelligent computers for geography teaching', in: *Geographical Association handbook on computers in geography teaching,* eds. Shepherd, I. & Walker, W. (forthcoming).

Ennals, J. R. (1984i) 'Computers and history', in: *Teaching History,* journal of the History Teachers Assoc. of New South Wales, April 1984.

Ennals, J. R. & Briggs, J. H. (1984a) 'Logic and Programming', in: ed. Torrance, S. *The mind and the machine,* Ellis Horwood.

Ennals, J. R. & Briggs, J. H. (1984b) 'Fifth Generation Computing: Introducing micro-PROLOG into the classroom', in: *Journal of Educational Computing Research,* 1 (No. 1).

Ennals, J. R., Briggs, J. H., & Brough, D. R. (1984) 'What the naive user requires of PROLOG', in: ed. Campbell, J. *Implementations of PROLOG,* Ellis Horwood.

Ennals, J. R., Bergman, M. & Boucelma, O. (1984) 'The French connection', in: ed. Ramsden, E. *Microcomputers in Education 2,* Ellis Horwood.

Fleck, J. (1982) 'Development and establishment in artificial intelligence', in: eds. Elias, N., Matins, H., & Whitley, R. Scientific Establishments and hierarchies, *Sociology of the sciences,* VI Reidel.

Floud, R. (1973) *An introduction to quantitative methods for historians,* Methuen.

Flugel, J. C. (1963) 'On the character and married life of Henry VIII', in: ed. Mazlish, B. *Psychoanalysis and history,* Prentice-Hall.

Fogel, R. W. (1973) 'Railroads as an analogy to the space effort: some economic aspects', in: eds Drake, M. *Applied historical studies,* Methuen.

Foucault, M. (1967) *Madness and Civilization,* Tavistock.

Foucault, M. (1970) *The Order of Things,* Tavistock.

Foucault, M. (1972) *The Archaeology of Knowledge,* Tavistock.

Foucault, M. (1973) *The Birth of the Cinic,* Tavistock.

Francis, J. (1983) *Microcomputers and teaching history,* Longman.

Fuchi, K. (1981) *Aiming for knowledge information processing systems,* Electrotechnical Laboratory, Ibaraki, Japan, and in: eds. Warren, D. & Van Caneghem, M. *Logic programming and its applications,* Ablex.

Gagne, R. M. (1967) *The conditions of learning,* Holt, Reinhardt & Winston.

Gagne, R. M. (1975) *Essentials of learning for instruction,* Holt, Reinhardt & Winston.

Gardiner, P. (1961) *The nature of historical explanation,* Oxford Univ. Press.

Giddens, A. (1976) *New rules of sociological method,* Hutchinson.

Godel, K. (1944) 'Russell's mathematical logic', in: ed. Schlepp, P. *The philosophy of Bertrand Russel,* Northern Univ. Press 123–153.

Goldberg, A. (1979) 'Educational uses of a dynabook', in: *Computers and Education,* 3 (no. 4).

Goldstein, I. P. (1975) 'Summary of MYCROFT: a system for understanding simple picture programs, *Artificial Intelligence,* 6 249–288.

Goodyear, P. (1984) *LOGO: A guide to learning through Programming,* Ellis Horwood.

Green, C. C. (1969) 'Theorem proving by resolution as a basis for question-answering systems, *Machine Intelligence 4,* Edinburgh University Press.

Guenoche, A. & Hesnard, A. (1982) *Typologie d'amphores Romaines par une methode logique classification,* LISH Marseilles.

Hallam, K. N. (1970) 'Piaget and thinking history', in: ed. Ballard, M. *New movements in the study and teaching of history,* Temple Smith.

Hammond, P. (1980) 'Logic programming for expert systems' MSc thesis Dept. of Computing, Imperial College.

Hammond, P. (1982a) APES: *A PROLOG expert system shell,* Dept. of Computing, Imperial College.

Hammond, P. (1982b) *APES user manual,* Imperial College DOC report 82/9.

Hammond, P. (1983) *Representation of DHSS regulations as a logic program,* DOC report 82/56 Imperial College.

Hammond, P. (1984) *CHIMP user manual* Imperial College.

Harre, R. (1974) 'Blueprint for a new science' in: ed. Armistead, N. *Reconstructing social psychology,* Penguin.

Hartley, J. R. (1981a) 'Learner initiatives in computer assisted learning', in: eds. Howe, J. A. M. & Ross, P. *Microcomputers in secondary education,* Kogan Page.

Hartley, J. R. (1981b) 'An appraisal of computer-assisted learning in the UK', in: ed. Rushby, N. J. *Selected readings in computer-based learning,* Kogan Page.

Hawkins, D. (1981) *An analysis of expert thinking,* Schlumberger-Doll Research, Ridgefield Connecticut USA.

Van Heijenoort, J. (ed) (1967) *From Frege to Godel,* Harvard Univ. Press.

Heines, J. H., Briggs, J. H. & Ennals, J. R. (1983) 'Logic and recursion: the PROLOG twist', *Creative Computing* November 1983.

Henin, B. (1983) *Les loyers Marseillais du XVIIeme Siecle avec le logiciel MICROBASE* HMCI No. 2 LISH/CNRS Marseilles.

Hewitt, C. (1972) *Description and theoretical analysis of PLANNER,* AI Memo 231 MIT Project MAC.

Hirst, P. H. (1973) 'Liberal education and the nature of knowledge', in: ed. Peters, R. S. *The philosophy of education,* Oxford Univ. Press.

Howe, J. A. M. (1978a) 'Artificial intelligence and computer-assisted learning: ten years on, *Programmed Learning and Educational Technology,* **15** (2) 114–125, and in: ed. Rushby, N. J. *Selected readings in computer-based learning,* Kogan Page.

Howe, J. A. M. (1978b) 'Using technology to educate pupils with communication difficulties', *THE Journal,* 5, 36–39.

Howe, J. A. M. (1978c) 'Developmental stages in learning to program', *DAI Research Paper No. 119,* Univ. of Edinburgh.

Howe, J. A. M. (1979a) 'Learning through model building', in: ed. Michie, D. *Expert systems in the microelectronic age,* Edinburgh Univ. Press.

Howe, J. A. M. & Du Boulay, B. (1979) 'Microprocessor assisted learning: turning the clock back?', *DAI Research paper No. 114,* Univ. of Edinburgh.

Howe, J. A. M., O'Shea, T. & Plane, F. (1979) 'Teaching mathematics through LOGO programming: an evaluation study', *DAI Research paper No. 115,*

Univ. of Edinburgh.

Howe, J. A. M., Ross, P. M., Johnson, K. R., Plane, F. & Inglis, R. (1981) 'Teaching mathematics through programming in the classroom, *DAI Research paper No. 157* Univ. of Edinburgh.

Howe, J. A. M. & Ross, P. M. (1981) 'Moving LOGO into a mathematics class-room', in: eds. Howe, J. A. M. & Ross, P. M. *Microcomputers in secondary education,* Kogan Page.

Hunt, J. (1979) *Computers in secondary school history teaching,* Historical Association.

Hurst, R. (1984) 'An information technology course using PROLOG', in: ed. Ramsden, E. *Microcomputers in Education 2,* Ellis Horwood.

ICOT (1982) Institute for New Generation Computer technology. *Outline of research and development plans for fifth generation computer systems.*

Julian, S. (1982) 'Graphics in micro-PROLOG', MSc thesis Dept. of Computing, Imperial College.

Kanoui, H. (1982) *PROLOG II Manual of examples,* Groupe Intelligence Artifi-cielle, Univ. of Aix-Marseille, Luminy.

Kanoui, H. & Van Caneghem, M. (1980) *Implementing a very high-level langauge on a very low-cost computer,* Groupe Intelligence Artificielle, Univ. of Aix-Marseille, Luminy.

Kelly, G. A. (1955) *The psychology of personal constructs,* Newton.

Kemmis, S. *et al.* (1977) *How children learn,* Centre for Applied Research in Education, Univ. of East Anglia.

King, T. J., Jardine, C. J. (1980) The use of a relational database management system to store historical records. 2nd International Conference on the use of Databases in the Humanities and Social Sciences, Madrid.

Kowalski, R. A. (1974) 'Predicate logic as programming language', *Proc. IFIP,* 569–574 North-Holland.

Kowalski, R. A. (1979) *Logic for problem solving,* Elsevier North-Holland.

Kowalski, R. A. (1982a) 'Logic as a computer language for children, invited lecture at *European Conference on Artificial Intelligence,* Orsay 1982, and in: ed. Yazdani, M. *New Horizons in educational computing,* Ellis Horwood (1984).

Kowalski, R. A. (1982b) 'Logic programming in the fifth generation, *Pergamon State of the Art Workshop on Fifth Generation Computer Systems.*

Kowalski, R. A. (1982c) 'Logic as a computer language', in: eds Clark, K. L. & Tarnlund, S-A. *Logic programming,* Academic Press.

Kowalski, R. A. (1983) *Logic and belief,* Department of Computing, Imperial College (revised version of Ch. 13 of *Logic for problem solving,* (Kowalski 1979).)

Kowalski, R. A. & Van Emden, M. (1976) The semantics of predicate logic as programming language, *JACM* **23,** (4) 733–743.

Kriwaczek, F. R. (1982) 'Some applications of PROLOG to decision support systems', MSc thesis, Depart. of Computing, Imperial College.

Kuhn, T. (1970) The Structure of Scientific Revolutions, Chicago University Press.

Labbett, B. D. C. (1977) *The local history classroom project 1975/1977,* CET 1977.

Lakates, I. (1976) *Proofs and Refutations: The logic of Mathematical Discovery,* Cambridge University Press.

Laslett, P. (1965) *The world we have lost* Methuen.

Laslett, P. (1977) *Family life and illicit love in earlier generations* Cambridge Univ. Press.

Latham, J. O. (1984) 'PROLOG and English teaching', in: ed. Ramsden, E. *Microcomputers in Education 2,* Ellis Horwood.

Leach, E. (1970) *Levi-Strauss,* Fontana.

Levi-Strauss, C. (1963) *Structural anthropology,* Basic Books.

Levi-Strauss C. (1969) *Elementary structures of kinship,* Eyre & Spottiswood.

Lighthill, J. (1972) *Artificial intelligence,* report to the Science Research Council.

Macfarlane, A. (1977) *Reconstructing historical communities* – records of *an English village: Earls Colne 1400–1750,* Cambridge Univ. Press.

Macfarlane, A. (1978) *The origins of English individualism,* Blackwell.

Mackie, J. L. (1974) *The cement of the universe: a study of causation,* Oxford Univ. Press.

Mackinolty, J. (ed.) (1983) *Past continuous,* History Teachers Assoc. of Australia.

McCabe, F. G. (1980) *micro-PROLOG programmer's reference manual.* Logic Programming Associates.

McCabe, F. G. (1982) *The Abstract PROLOG machine,* Dept. of Computing Imperial College.

McCarthy, J. (1982) *The map colouring problem and the Kowalski doctrine,* Standford Univ. AI Lab.

McCarthy, J., Abrahams, P. W., Edwards, D. J., Hart, J. P. & Lewin, M. I. (1962) *LISP programmers manual,* MIT Press.

Murakami, K. (1983) 'Archery discipline and fifth generation research', *ICOT Journal,* No. 2 Tokyo.

Mylopoulos, J. (1980) 'An overview of knowledge representation', *ACM proc Workshop on Data Abstraction, Databases and Conceptual Modelling,* eds. Brodie, M. L., Zillies, S. N.

Naish, L. (1982) 'An Introduction to MU-PROLOG', *Technical Report 82/2,* Dept. of Computer Science, Univ. of Melbourne.

Nichol, J. (1979) *The Saxons,* Blackwell.

Nichol, J. (1980) *Simulation in history teaching: a practical approach,* Historical Association.

Nichol, J. & Dean, J. (1984a) 'Pupils, computers and history teaching', in: ed. Yazdani, M. *New Horizons in educational computing,* Ellis Horwood.

Nichol, J. & Dean, J. (1984b) 'Computers and children's historical thinking and understanding, presented at *Sussex Conference on AI, Education and Child Development, July 1984,* Sussex Univ.

Nichol, J. & Dean, J. (1984c) *Classroom based curriculum development: artificial intelligence and history teaching,* School of Education, Exeter Univ.

Nichol, J., Dean, J., Tompsett, C. & Briggs, J. (1984) 'Computing for Everyman or computer applications in micro-PROLOG', in: ed. Ramsden, E., *Micro-*

computers in Education 2, Ellis Horwood.

O'Shea, T. (1981) 'A self-improving quadratic tutor', in: eds. Sleeman, D. & Brown, J. S. *Intelligent tutoring systems,* Academic Press.

O'Shea, T. & Self, J. (1983) *Learning and teaching with computers,* Harvester.

Orwell, G. (1948) *1984* Penguin.

Orwell, G. (1957) 'Politics *vs* literature: An examination of *Gulliver's Travels'* 'Politics and the English language' 'The prevention of literature' 'Boys Weeklies', in: *Inside the whale and other essays,* Penguin.

Orwell, G. (1962) *The road to Wigan Pier, Penguin.*

Papert, S. (1980) *Mindstorms,* Basic Books and Harvester.

Papert, S. & Solomon, C. (1971) 'Twenty things to do with a computer', *AI Memo No. 248,* MIT AI Lab.

Papert, S., Watt, D., Di Sessa, A. & Weir, S. (1979) *Final Report of the Brookline LOGO Project,* MIT AI Lab.

Parkinson, G. H. R. (1968) *The theory of meaning,* Oxford Univ. Press.

Parsons, T. (1937) *The structure of social action,* McGraw-Hill.

Pasero, R. (1982) 'A dialogue in natural language', in: *Proc. First International Logic Programming Conference,* ed. Van Caneghem, M. 1982.

Pask, G. (1970) 'Computer assisted learning and instruction', in: eds. Annett, J. & Duke, J., *Proc. seminar on Computer-Based Learning systems,* Leeds.

Pask, G. (1981) 'Entailment meshes as representation of knowledge and learning', in: eds. Howe, J. A. M. & Ross, P. *Microcomputers in secondary education,* Kogan Page.

Pask, G. & Curran, S. (1982) *Microman,* Century, London.

Pask, G. & Scott, B. C. E. (1972) 'Learning strategies and individual competence', *International Journal of Man-Machine Studies,* **4**, 217–253.

Peel, E. A. (1960) *The pupil's thinking,* Oldbourne.

Peel, E. A. (1967) 'Some problems in the psychology of history teaching, in: eds. Burston, W. H. and Thompson, D. *Studies in the nature and teaching of history,* Routledge Kegan Paul.

Piaget, J. (1926) *The language and thought of the child,* Routledge Kegan Paul.

Piaget, J. (1928) *Judgement and reasoning in the child,* Routledge Kegan Paul.

Piaget, J. (1950) *The psychology of intelligence,* Routledge Kegan Paul.

Piaget, J. (1970) *Psychology and epistemology,* Penguin.

Piaget, J. (1971) *Structuralism,* Routledge Kegan Paul.

Piaget, J. & Inhelder, B. (1958) *The growth of logical thinking from childhood to adolescence,* Basic Books.

Pique, J. F. (1982) 'On a semantic representation of natural language sentences', in: *Proc. First International Logic Programming Conference,* ed. Van Caneghem, M.

Pitt-Rivers, J. A. (1971) *The people of the Sierra* Chicago.

Popper, K. R. (1945) *The open society and its enemies,* Routledge Kegan Paul.

Richards, T. (1983) *Teaching logic with PROLOG,* La Trobe University, Melbourne.

Ridd, S. (1982) 'An investigation of PROLOG as an aid to French teaching and language translation', BSc thesis Dept. of Computing, Imperial College.

Robinson, J. A. (1965) 'A machine oriented logic based on the resolution principle', *JACM,* **12,** 23–41.

Robinson, J. A. (1968) 'Hume's two definitions of "Cause" ', in: ed. Chappell, V. C. Hume.

Robinson, J. A. (1979a) *Logic: form and function. The mechanisation of deductive reasoning,* Edinburgh Univ. Press.

Robinson, J. A. (1979b) 'The logical basis of programming by assertion and query', in: ed. Michie, D. *Expert systems in the microelectronic age,* Edinburgh Univ. Press.

Robinson, J. A. (1983) 'Logical reasoning in machines', in: eds. Hayes, J. E. & Michie, D. *Intelligent systems,* Ellis Horwood.

Robinson, J. A. (1984) *Logic programming – past, present and future* ICOT.

Robinson, J. A. & Sibert, E. E. (1981) *LOGLISP: motivation, design and implementation,* Syracuse Univ.

Robinson, J. A. & Sibert, E. E. (1982) 'LOGLISP: an alternative to PROLOG', in: eds Hayes, J. E., Michie, D. & Pao, Y. H. *Machine Intelligence 10,* Ellis Horwood.

Rogers, P. J. (1975) 'Some philosophical aspects of curriculum construction with special reference to history, PhD thesis Univ. of Glasgow.

Rogers, P. J. (1978) *The new history,* Historical Association.

Ross, P. (1980) 'Computers in education' *Occasional Paper No. 17* DAI Univ. of Edinburgh.

Ross, P. (1983) *LOGO Programming,* Addison-Wesley.

Ross, P. J. & Howe, J. A. M. (1979) *Teaching mathematics through programming: ten years on,* DAI Univ. of Edinburgh.

Roussel, P. (1975) *PROLOG: manuel de reference et d'utilisation* Groupe intelligence artificielle Univ of Aix-Marseille, Luminy.

Rushby, N. J. (1979) *An Introduction to educational computing,* Croom Helm.

Rushby, N. J. (1981) 'Educational innovation and computer-based learning' in: ed. Rushby, N. J. *Selected readings in computer-based learning',* Kogan Page.

Ryle, A. (1975) *Frames and cages,* Sussex Univ. Press.

Sage, M. & Smith, D. (1983) Microcomputers in Education Social Science Research Council.

Santane-Toth, E. & Szeredi, P. (1982) 'PROLOG applications in Hungary', in eds. Clark, K. L. & Tarnlund, S-A Academic Press.

Schank, R. (1982) Invited lecture at *European Conference on Aritificial Intelligence,* Orsay.

Screen, S. (1978) 'Census data interrogation', *Project paper 12 Computers in the Curriculum Schools Council.*

Self, J. A. (1979) 'Student models and artificial intelligence' *Computers and Education,* **3,** (4).

Self, J. A. (forthcoming) *The Unholy Grail of educational computing.*

Sergot, M. (1982) 'Prospects for representing the law as logic programs' in: eds. Clark, K. L. & Tarnlund, S-A. *Logic programming,* Academic Press.

Sergot, M. (1983) 'A query-the-user facility for logic programming', in: eds.

Dagano, P. & Sandewall, E. *Integrated interative computing systems,* North-Holland, and in: ed. Yazdani, M. *New horizons in educational computing,* Ellis Horwood.

Shaw, M. L. G. (1979) 'Personal learning through the computer', *Computers and Education,* **3**, (4).

Shemilt, D. (1980) *History 13–16 evaluation study,* Holmes MacDougall.

Shemilt, D. (1984) 'The Devil's locomotive', in: eds. Dickinson, A. & Lee, P. J.

Shorter, E. (1971) *The historian and the computer: a practical guide,* Prentice-Hall.

Shortliffe, E. H. (1978) *Computer-based medical consultations: MYCIN,* North-Holland Elsevier.

Simon, H. (1969) *The sciences of the artificial,* MIR Press.

Sloman, A. (1978) *The Computer Revolution in Philosophy,* Harvester.

Stansfield, J. L. (1974) 'Programming a dialogue teaching situation', PhD dissertation, School of AI, Univ. of Edinburgh.

Steel, B. D. (1981) 'Expert- the implementation of a data-independent expert system with quasi-natural language information input', *Research report DOC 81/23,* Imperial College.

Suppes, P. (1979) 'Current trends in computer-assisted instruction', *Advances in Computers,* **18**, Academic Press.

Suppes, P. & Morningstar, M. (1972) *Computer-assisted instruction at Stanford,* Academic Press.

Tallon, W., Ball, D. & Tomley, D. (1982) 'BASIC or PROLOG: choosing the right language for a biology teaching task'. *Computers in Schools,* **5**, (1).

Thorne, M. (1981) 'Real computer studies', *Educational Computing,* October.

Torrance, S. (1983) *Thinking through PROLOG,* Middlesex Polytechic.

Torrance, S. (ed) (1984) *The mind and the machine,* Ellis Horwood.

Turing, A. M. (1950) 'Computing machinery and intelligence', in: *Mind* October 1950 **59**, 433–460, and in: eds. Feigenbaum, E. A. & Feldman, J. *Computers and thought,* McGraw-Hill.

Turner, D. (1971) *Historical demography in schools,* Historical Association.

Vogel, C. (1983a) *POC-POC* University of La Reunion.

Vogel, C. (1983b) *Language and creativity: the Creole connection,* University of La Reunion.

Wallace, M. (1984) *Communicating with databases in natural language,* Ellis Horwood.

Warren, D. H. D. (1982) 'Higher-order extensions to PROLOG: are they needed?', in: eds. Hayes, J. E., Michie, D. & Pao, Y. H. *Machine Intelligence 10,* Ellis Horwood.

Warren D. H. D. & Pereira, F. L. N. 'An efficient easily adaptable system for interpreting natural language queries (CHAT-80)' *DAI Research paper No. 155,* Univ. of Edinburgh.

Warren, D. & Van Caneghem, M. (eds) (1984) *Logic programming and its applications,* Ablex.

Watson, G. (1962) *The literary critics,* Penguin.

Weber, M. (1949) *Max Weber on the methodology of the social sciences,* Glencoe, The Free Press.

Weir, D. J. (1982) 'Teaching Logic programming: an interactive approach', MSc thesis, Dept. of Computing, Imperial College.

Weir, S. (1981) LOGO as an information prosthetic for the handicapped' *DSRE Working paper 9,* MIT.

Weir, S. & Emmanuel, R. (1976) 'Using LOGO to catalyse communication in an autistic child', *DAI Research report No. 15,* Univ. of Edinburgh.

Weizenbaum, J. (1966) 'ELIZA − A computer program for the study of natural language communication between man and machine', Comm ACM **9**, (1) 39−45.

Weizenbaum, J. (1976) *Computer power and human reason,* Freeman.

Wheeler, M. (1943) *Maiden Castle,* London.

Wilks, Y. (1976) 'Frames, scripts, stories and fantasies', *International Conference on Psychology of Language,* Univ. of Stirling.

Wilks, Y. & Bien, J. (1981) *Beliefs, points of view and multiple environments* CSCM-6 Univ. of Essex.

Winch, P. (1958) *The idea of a social science,* Routledge Kegan Paul.

Winograd, T. (1972) *Understanding natural language,* Edinburgh Univ. Press.

Winston, P. H. & Horn, B. K. (1981) *LISP,* Addison-Wesley.

Wittgenstein, L. (1968) *Philosophical investigations,* Blackwell.

Wolsk, D. (ed.) (1975) 'An experience-centred curriculum: exercises in perception, communication and action, *Educational Studies and Documents No. 17,* UNESCO.

Wood, E. S. (1979) *Archaeology in Britain, Collins field guide,* Collins.

Von Wright, G. H. (1971) *Explanation and understanding,* London.

Yazdani, M. (ed.) (1984) *New horizons in educational computing,* Ellis Horwood.

Index